Who Killed Diana?

Peter Hounam and Derek McAdam

 Frog, Ltd.
Berkeley, California

 VISION Paperbacks
London, England

To Liz

Who Killed Diana?

ISBN 1-883319-87-0

Published by Frog, Ltd.

Frog, Ltd. books are distributed by
North Atlantic Books
P.O. Box 12327
Berkeley, CA 94712

First published in Great Britain in 1998 by VISION Paperbacks, a divi-sion of Satin Publications Limited, 20 Queen Anne Street, London W1M 0AY, E-mail: 100557.1745@compuserve.com.

Photography: Rex Features Ltd.
Design and layout: Justine Hounam

Printed in the United States of America

Distributed to the book trade by Publishers Group West

1 2 3 4 5 6 7 8 9 / 02 01 00 99 98

Who
Killed
Diana?

Contents

The Authors

Peter Hounam

As one of Britain's best-known investigative journalists, Peter Hounam has studied murder and corruption in many countries. With The Sunday Times Insight Team he broke the story of Mordechai Vanunu, the Israeli nuclear whistle-blower. Last year he exposed the dangerous world of international cigarette smuggling for BBC Television. In 1997 he won the What-The-Papers-Say, Scoop of the Year Award. He is 54 and his last book was an exposé of South Africa's nuclear weapons program.

Derek McAdam

Born in North London in 1938, Derek McAdam was a financial journalist working in the City. He trained on the Stock Exchange Gazette, where he was news editor for many years before joining the financial team on *The Sun*. Later he moved to the *Sunday Express* as a Financial Feature Writer. Eventually after 20 years he moved to Scotland where he became a hotelier on the Isle of Mull while writing regularly for both local and national newspapers.

Introduction

The picture of Diana, Princess of Wales, leaping joyfully aboard a launch in the bay at St. Tropez, arms stretched wide in exhilaration, swept around the world. A brief moment in a brief holiday in an equally brief romance, it encapsulated all the newfound happiness of the troubled Princess.

For newspapers and their readers, it was an exciting moment. The world's press had discovered early on that pictures of Diana equalled higher sales and enhanced profits.

Suddenly it seemed a whole new episode, bursting with opportunities, was opening in her life. This was an episode which would provide the press with the greatest opportunities of all — the possibility of a romance with a good-looking, vastly wealthy Arab. He was a lover with an 'interesting' past and playboy reputation whose famous father had suffered constant rejections by the British authorities.

The story was hot and the newspapers were prepared to pay big money for pictures. In the overheated atmosphere of those heady days the professional snappers, proud of the title 'paparazzi,' were happily anticipating a bonanza.

Fortunes had been made from intimate unauthorized pictures of the Duchess of York. A secret romance for the Princess of Wales promised an earnings spree the likes of which had never been seen before.

For another group of observers the prospect was altogether less exciting. The British Establishment had viewed the Princess as a loose cannon for a long time. Now it seemed the cannon was about to explode in the most disastrous way.

It is difficult to pinpoint the exact moment when 'Shy Di' turned into 'Feisty Di,' but it was a change that alarmed the Royal family, their senior advisors, and the higher echelons of the British Government.

It was bad enough that her natural talent for public relations had overwhelmed the reticence of Prince Charles. It was a serious worry that she had become the brilliant figurehead of a worldwide movement against land mines and in the process had upset the powerful lobby of the international military/industrial complex and was sending ripples through the precarious balance of international relations.

But infinitely worse was the prospect that the Princess might become involved with the son of an unpopular Egyptian billionaire with a tarnished reputation. For the Establishment every implication of the association was alarming.

The scenario opening in front of their horrified eyes was of a possible marriage to an Egyptian playboy followed almost inevitably by a conversion to Islam. It was unthinkable that the heir to the throne and his younger brother should have a Muslim stepfather.

It was equally unthinkable that the union might produce an Anglo/Egyptian half-brother for the royal Princes. Links with European Royalty had been the norm for many generations — but an association with an Arab businessman whose fortune had a questionable provenance was a horse of a different color.

Somewhere between these two disparate groups — the media and the Establishment — and a driver apparently high on drink and drugs, lies the truth behind the death of the 'People's Princess.' This book aims to get close to the answer.

The French investigating authorities and the British Government have said from the beginning there was no conspiracy. But in the words of Mandy Rice-Davies, that other young lady who embarrassed the Establishment a generation earlier, 'They would [say that] wouldn't they?'

We examine and analyze compelling new evidence that while the aggressive attentions of the paparazzi must have had a direct influence on the crash which killed the Princess and Dodi Fayed, and while the car's driver may have had too much to drink, there were other secret, sinister forces at work which may ultimately prove that there was indeed a conspiracy.

It is human nature to want simple straightforward answers to baffling questions, but the crash in the Paris tunnel may never be fully explained. The apparent incompetence of the French authorities in failing to control the crash scene, in not finding some of the most important witnesses, and in selectively leaking some information while maintaining iron secrecy over much of their investigation has contributed to a widespread belief that a cover-up is in progress.

If, as expected, the official conclusion is that Henri Paul, Dodi and Diana's driver, was drunk and therefore lost control of his car, the speculation will continue, just as so many people still believe Lee Harvey Oswald was not the lone assassin of President John Kennedy in Dallas.

Whichever standpoint one takes, there is one certainty about the tragic deaths of Diana, Princess of Wales, Dodi Fayed, and Henri Paul, and the maiming of guard Trevor Rees-Jones: someone, or some unidentified group, was responsible for the terrible crash of their Mercedes limousine.

It was not an unavoidable act of fate, an accident that could happen to any of us. Either Henri Paul was to blame for being drunk and speeding out of control—with his employers facing searching questions about why he was allowed to be drunk on duty—or unidentified assassins planned a hit that was engineered to look like an unfortunate pileup.

The idea of a group of killers premeditatedly wiping out one of the most famous people in the world and her lover is surely so unlikely as to be instantly dismissed, but this book urges caution in that regard. The evidence that renegade groups loyal to the British Establishment and the Royal Family are prepared to operate outside the law is rarely discussed in the newspapers. However, as we show, there are indeed such groups and the people they represent were acutely concerned at the direction Diana's life was taking.

'Dear me!' people may cry, 'this is yet another conspiracy theory,' and they will feel inclined to dismiss the arguments on that score alone. The writer Jeffrey M. Bale has examined this tendency in professional researchers and he too urges people not to jump too easily to the simplest, most acceptable conclusion.

Bale writes: 'Very few notions generate as much intellectual resistance, hostility, and derision within academic circles as a belief in the historical importance or efficacy of political conspiracies. Even when this belief is expressed in a very cautious manner, limited to specific and restricted contexts, supported by reliable evidence, and hedged about with all sort of qualifications, it still manages to transcend the boundaries of acceptable discourse and violate unspoken academic taboos.

'The idea that particular groups of people meet together secretly or in private to plan various courses of action, and that some of these plans actually exert a significant influence on particular historical developments, is typically rejected out of hand and assumed to be the figment of a paranoid imagination.

'The mere mention of the word "conspiracy" seems to set off an internal alarm bell which causes scholars to close their minds in order to avoid cognitive dissonance and possible unpleasantness, since the popular image of conspiracy both fundamentally challenges the conception most educated, sophisticated people have about how the world operates and reminds them of the horrible persecutions that absurd and unfounded conspiracy theories have precipitated or sustained in the past.'

Readers are therefore urged to keep an open mind about the key questions, whatever the French investigative team has concluded. Was there a cover-up by the Ritz? Was a shadowy group out to protect the Royal Family at all costs? Was there a contract out on the life of Dodi? Did someone tamper with the Mercedes and was its driver poisoned?

The first mutterings of such perfectly valid conspiracy theories were portrayed by the media as contemptible, perhaps reflecting a grieving public's disgust that the questions were actually being raised. But was this a true reflection of the public's attitude towards the crash? When dealing with such a sensitive issue, it is difficult to judge whether the media was simply reflecting public opinion or whether press and television were shaping a stance on the crash with which they thought the public should agree.

As the months have passed, there are signs that a more objective approach has been adopted. Now that the dust has long since settled in the Pont de L'Alma tunnel, the time is right to put aside sentimental worries and look at the facts and inconsistencies in evidence with a sharp eye.

We would like to thank the many people in France, Germany, Britain, and the United States who have contributed to our research and who have sometimes taken a professional risk to talk to us. Many of them share the view that the truth of what happened in Paris has not come out and that the full range of options need to be considered unfettered by prejudice.

This is a book for those who would prefer to know.

Chronology

JUNE 3, 1997 Mohammed Al Fayed invites Diana, Princess of Wales, to join his family on holiday at their villa near St. Tropez.

JUNE 11 Diana formally accepts the invitation.

JULY 14 Holiday party leave Britain by Harrods Gulfstream IV executive jet for Nice, where they board the 140-foot luxury motor yacht *Jonikal* for the voyage along the Mediterranean coast to St. Tropez.

JULY 15 Dodi leaves girlfriend Kelly Fisher in Paris to join holiday party in St. Tropez.

JULY 20 Holiday ends and Diana flies back to London with Prince William and Prince Harry. Dodi and Kelly continue sailing on the yacht *Cujo.*

JULY 23 Dodi and Kelly arrive in Nice and fly to Paris. Kelly leaves for Los Angeles the next day.

JULY 25	Diana and Dodi arrive at Paris Ritz for a romantic weekend.
JULY 27	The couple returns to London.
JULY 31	Diana and Dodi leave for six-day holiday cruising on the yacht *Jonikal* in the Mediterranean, visiting Corsica and Sardinia.
AUGUST 4	Photographer Mario Brenna takes pictures of Diana and Dodi kissing on the deck of the *Jonikal,* which sell for more than £1 million ($1.65 million).
AUGUST 6	The couple returns to London.
AUGUST 7	Diana dines at Dodi's apartment in Park Lane, overlooking Hyde Park.
AUGUST 8	Diana leaves for Bosnia in support of Landmine Survivors Network.
AUGUST 10	Diana returns to London to find 11 pages of pictures of herself and Dodi kissing on the *Jonikal.* The couple leaves London for the Al Fayed estate at Oxted, Surrey.
AUGUST 12	Diana and Dodi visit clairvoyant Rita Rogers at her home near Chesterfield, Derbyshire, traveling by Harrods helicopter.
AUGUST 13	Diana leaves Oxted for Kensington Palace and that night she and Dodi enjoy a night on the town in London—Diana gets home at 2 A.M.

AUGUST 14	Diana spends evening at Dodi's apartment, arriving home in the early hours of the morning.
AUGUST 15	Diana leaves London for a holiday in Greece with her friend Rosa Monckton. They travel by Harrods executive jet.
AUGUST 20	Diana arrives back in London and has dinner with Dodi at the Park Lane apartment.
AUGUST 21	Diana and Dodi leave London on the Al Fayed Gulfstream IV jet for Nice, where they board the *Jonikal* for a Mediterranean cruise.
AUGUST 22	*Jonikal* arrives in Monte Carlo and the couple visit jeweler Alberto Repossi to look at rings.
AUGUST 30	The holiday cruise comes to an end and the couple flies to Paris to visit the Windsor villa on the Bois de Boulogne and to stay overnight at Dodi's apartment just off the rue Champs Elysées. Dodi visits Alberto Repossi to collect the ring.
	Diana telephones journalist Richard Kay from the Paris Ritz to tell him she intended to withdraw from public life in November.
AUGUST 31	The couple leaves the Paris Ritz shortly after midnight to return to the flat near the Champs Elysées in the Mercedes. The crash occurs at 12.25 A.M. in the tunnel under the Place de L'Alma.

Chapter One

Romance in the Sun

t is a well-known irony that Diana, Princess of Wales, the 'People's Princess,' was loved throughout much of the world for her warmth and compassion, but she rarely experienced those emotions during her childhood. As a youngster she often felt rejected and even abandoned as she traveled forlornly between one parent and another and between schools and houses which while beautiful rarely offered a warm and loving refuge. She was a lively child with a healthy sense of mischief, a deep love for her younger brother, and respect for her elder sisters, but there was nevertheless a melancholy about her which is apparent in many of her earliest photographs.

Contrast these early pictures with those taken during the last months of her life, particularly those taken during the holiday she spent with the Al Fayed family in the summer of 1997, at their villa overlooking the Mediterranean at St. Tropez. These pictures, many taken by the paparazzi who dominated so much of her adult life, show a radiantly happy woman, relaxed in the company of her sons and the extended Al Fayed family.

A beautiful, confident, and genuinely contented woman at the height of her powers shines through in every picture of

Diana, alone with Dodi on the cruises around the Sardinian coast aboard the *Jonikal*. She was loved for presenting the world with a perfect image of a stylishly elegant Princess, and additionally she was respected for the energy and commitment she gave to her charitable causes, for her hands-on approach, and the time she devoted to visiting the terminally ill in hospitals wherever she went.

For Diana, it was a long and troubled journey from a disrupted childhood to reach the respect, recognition, and bliss that she found in those final months. Suggestions that the obvious empathy between the Princess and Dodi Fayed stemmed from shared childhood experiences could be close to the truth: both were born into wealthy and privileged families where the father was often little more than a distant figure. Both suffered from a breakdown in their parents' marriages, and both experienced emotional damage when their mothers left home.

Following their parents' divorces, both Diana and Dodi's fathers gained custody of their children, in contrast to the prevailing customs. To both it had perhaps appeared to represent a desertion by their mothers at an impressionable age. In the end, these similarities in childhood experience were eminently capable of overcoming all of the cultural and religious differences between the two.

Diana and her younger brother Charles, now the 9th Earl Spencer, were devastated by the breakdown of their parents' marriage. This could only have been made worse by the separation coinciding with the departure of Sarah and Jane (the two elder Spencer girls) for boarding school. The Spencer children's background was essentially one of aristocratic wealth and privilege, lacking nothing in the way of material needs.

At Christmas they were sometimes given catalogs from

Hamleys, the famous toy store in London's Regent Street, and told to select the presents they would like Father Christmas to bring. Those presents would invariably be there on Christmas day, an experience which few children can boast. But despite all of this, their parents were essentially a distant image, occupying the same house but a seemingly different world, and only rarely seen from the nursery.

There were few hugs and kisses or outward displays of affection, which were longed for by both Diana and her brother, especially as the silences and growing hostility of the marriage's breakup filtered frighteningly into their young lives. Familiar as it may be today, at that time divorce was much less part of the normal domestic scene; at preparatory school Diana was the only girl in her year whose parents were separated.

As trial separation became full separation and subsequently divorce, family life became fragmented. The children were mostly away at school, with weekends divided between the parents. Visits to their mother at her new home in London's fashionable Belgravia, and later at her home on the Scottish Isle of Seil, were difficult. Diana was often in tears, upset even as they arrived that they would have to leave again the next day.

There was growing competition between the parents for the children's affections, and Diana was later to speak movingly of the problem she faced when both father and mother presented her with a new dress for a special occasion. Whichever dress she chose was bound to upset the other parent. Then there were difficulties with the constant stream of nannies through their young lives, some of whom provided comfort and friendship but many of whom could be casually cruel and uncaring.

Returning home from school, Diana and her brother would worry about what challenges the next young and pretty nanny, usually chosen by her father, would present. One beat their heads with a wooden spoon, another fed them laxatives as a punishment. Another nanny was so disliked by the children that they set pins in her chair to prick her when she sat down. Naughty but not exactly wicked perhaps, it was certainly a very clear statement of their feelings.

In the early days, Diana was inclined towards a little emotional blackmail regarding school, telling her father on one occasion that if he left her there it must mean that he didn't love her. Her schooldays were, however, for the most part quite happy and enjoyable. She enjoyed life at Riddlesworth Hall Preparatory School and later at West Heath boarding school in Sevenoaks, Kent, where both her sisters had preceded her. Diana particularly enjoyed sports, and was an enthusiastic competitor at swimming, netball, and hockey, while she also enjoyed tap and ballet dancing. As she was quite willing to admit later on, she was never going to be an academic.

Her failure to live up to the scholastic achievements of both her sisters and her brother was a worry to her, but even at that age, other abilities were emerging: while she was at West Heath, Diana's caring talents first revealed themselves during many visits to local hospitals and psychiatric wards. Family life continued to change—first her mother married Peter Shand Kydd, a development generally approved of by the children; and then her father married Raine, daughter of the novelist Barbara Cartland, then boasting the title Lady Lewisham (and later Countess of Dartmouth). Raine swept into the Spencer family like a storm, charming no one except 'Johnny' Spencer. With her autocratic ways she made instant enemies of all the children, earning herself the nickname Acid Raine.

There were other changes in the lives of the family, the

most significant being when the 7th Earl Spencer died in 1975 at the age of eighty-three. 'Johnny' Spencer became the 8th Earl, the children all inherited titles, and the family moved from the relatively homely Park House, in the shadow of Sandringham House (the Royal home in Norfolk), to the echoing spaces of the ancestral home, Althorp House, Northamptonshire. In addition to the title, the new Earl Spencer also inherited considerable debts.

This was not to affect the children's lives in any significant way, except for the overenthusiastic and unwelcome efforts of Raine, Lady Spencer, to open Althorp to the public, with a view to turning it into a money-making 'stately home.' Changes to the house and its outbuildings together with the sale of many valuable objects from Althorp during Raine's 'reign' caused considerable conflict between her and other members of the family.

After her formal schooling was complete, Diana followed her sisters to the Institut Alpin Videmanette, a Swiss finishing school for the daughters of the world's wealthy and famous. She hated just about everything at the Institut, and stayed for only one term. This was to prove another extraordinary link between her life and that of Dodi Fayed, who also had an abbreviated stay at a school for boys in nearby Gstaad. Leaving the Institut at the age of sixteen, Diana was considered too young to be let loose on her own in London, but she was not content to settle for the country life at Althorp.

Her eldest sister Sarah, at the time a leading figure on the London social scene, solved the problem by finding Diana work with her married friends, babysitting in return for a room and a pound an hour. This heralded the start of Diana's career in childcare, which she continued after she moved to London.

One job, found through a London agency, led to a lifelong

friendship with the Robertson family, whose baby son Patrick was looked after by Diana during the family's stay in London. The Robertsons remember the young Diana as a breath of fresh air in their house, lavishing love on the children and modestly quiet about her aristocratic background.

Before long, her father, to whom she had become closer over the years, purchased a London flat for his lively youngest daughter, which she shared with friends who were to become a major support to her in the events to come. It was at this time that the world was introduced to the shy teenager, scurrying from the nursery school to her prized Mini Metro, looking astonished at the attentions of the photographers who were soon to become a dominating feature in her life. Perhaps she genuinely could not understand what all the fuss was about.

If there had been melancholy and unhappiness during her childhood it was nothing compared to what came next. Early in the courtship with Prince Charles, Diana discovered the importance of Camilla Parker-Bowles in his life. Diana believed that there was genuine love between herself and the Prince during the early days of the marriage, but she was always aware of the menacing presence of the Prince's mistress, and as she was eventually to claim in the famous television interview, the three of them made for a 'crowded' marriage.

Diana had kept herself 'pure' in the old-fashioned sense for her marriage, and it was an important factor in her suitability as a Royal bride. What she needed more than anything else in her marriage was a close personal relationship, tactile and loving. It was to prove very difficult (if not impossible) for her husband, whose upbringing simply had not encompassed anything remotely approaching such intimacy.

For Diana, the combination of a remote and austere husband, together with his refusal to renounce his relationship with an older woman, led to well-publicized problems with bulimia and several suicide attempts. At the end of her marriage, the battles with the Palace over the terms of the divorce and worries that she might lose her children reduced the Princess to the lowest emotional ebb of her life. Throughout everything, her children were to provide both support and great happiness, and it is possible to postulate that many of the qualities of their mother have been passed to the Princes.

The ending of the marriage came eventually in August 1996 with the issue of a *decree nisi*. It was to be followed by yet another unsettled and unhappy period for the Princess as she searched for a new role in public life. It was still some time away from the point where Mohammed Al Fayed felt he could invite the Princess on a family holiday, but the contacts between the Spencer family and Al Fayed went back many years and Mohammed Al Fayed was to claim that he regarded Diana's father, the 8th Earl Spencer, as a brother.

It is widely acknowledged that Al Fayed had helped the 8th Earl during the worst of his financial problems. He in turn helped Mohammed with his naturalization problems. Diana was a regular customer at Al Fayed's famous store, Harrods in Knightsbridge, and Al Fayed told staff always to inform him of her presence so that he could come down to greet her. Her stepmother Raine was a director of the company. At one point, Al Fayed also invited the Princess of Wales to become a director, but she refused on the grounds that it would not have been an appropriate position for her to take.

Despite this, Diana continued to enjoy special status in the store, including an open account with unlimited purchasing powers; she was allowed in to browse and buy at times when the store was closed to other customers. She was also in the habit of popping in to Al Fayed's office in the store to chat over a cup of tea or coffee.

There were other contacts between Diana and Al Fayed quite separate from the pleasures and profits of shopping: Mohammed Al Fayed has been involved for many years in raising money for a wide variety of charities. It was inevitable that they would often find themselves supporting the same cause, and there were many meetings at charity balls, galas, and dinners. It was after one of these meetings that Al Fayed raised the subject of Diana, William, and Harry joining him, his wife Heini, and their four children on a holiday to the French Riviera.

Al Fayed had been pressing the Princess for some time to enjoy the family's hospitality at one of their many splendid homes around the world, but for many reasons it had never before been suitable or appropriate. This time, in the early summer of 1997, there appeared to be no such problems. The Princess had been considering a holiday in Thailand with her two boys, offered by multimillionaire businessman Gulu Lalvani, but the invitation from Mohammed Al Fayed to join his extended family now had more attraction.

The Al Fayed children were all around the same age as the Princes, and the protected villa close to the French Mediterranean resort of St. Tropez seemed to offer the perfect opportunity for relaxation and fun. There would also be the additional advantage of the enormous private yacht, the *Jonikal,* on which Al Fayed immediately spent £12 million ($19.8 million); the beautiful sailing yacht *Sakara;* the private Harrods jet; and the helicopter.

As a package holiday it offered luxury almost beyond the dreams of even royalty. So on July 11, 1997, almost a year after the unpleasantness of the divorce, Diana, with Princes William and Harry, climbed aboard the Harrods Gulfstream IV executive jet for the flight to Nice. Also on board were Mohammed and Heini Al Fayed and their children, two boys aged fourteen and ten, and two girls aged seventeen and twelve.

From Nice, the party was chauffeured to a nearby harbor where they boarded *Jonikal* for the voyage along the Mediterranean coast to Castel Ste. Hélène, the ten-acre Al Fayed estate on the exclusive Le Parc development overlooking the sparkling blue sea. The Princess and Princes were allocated their own luxurious eight-bedroom 'cottage' in the grounds.

The holiday was to last for ten days and was to launch a romance that was not so much a whirlwind as a tornado. From the day that Diana and Dodi met on the fourth day of the holiday, they were rarely to be apart until the day they died in the tunnel under the Pont de L'Alma in Paris.

At the beginning of Diana's holiday at Castel Ste. Hélène, Dodi was in Paris with his girlfriend of one year, Kelly Fisher, enjoying the Bastille Day celebrations along the Champs Elysées. A telephone call from his father sent Dodi scuttling off to join the party on the French Riviera, telling Kelly he had to go to London on business.

Although Kelly later joined him on the yachts *Sakara* and *Cujo* for part of the holiday, it was effectively the end of their relationship and heralded a period of bitter recrimination by the American model, including legal action for a 'breach of promise' allegation, and a torrid kiss-and-tell story sold for thousands of pounds to the British press. One of the more newsworthy allegations made by Kelly Fisher was that during the stay on the coast Dodi was sleeping with both her and the Princess and that he indulged in three-in-a-bed fantasies about the two women.

After the crash, Kelly was publicly to regret her actions at the time, although many people would no doubt have sympathies for anyone so abruptly expelled from the luxurious, jet-set lifestyle.

It took the paparazzi and other press photographers less than twenty-four hours to discover that the Princess and her sons were on holiday with the Al Fayed family, and soon there were fifty or more snappers and journalists crowded around the Castel Ste. Hélène. As the holiday progressed they were to become ever more intrusive, hiring launches to trail the party to the holiday yachts and a helicopter to hover over the estate.

Occasionally the Princess was able to deal with the press on a friendly basis and once or twice she put on a show for them, allowing them to do their work in the hope of a little peace later on. Sadly, the photographers did not see this as the way to pursue their business, and the relationship between the holiday-makers and the photographers became ever more fragile.

It was during this period that Mohammed Al Fayed called in extra security staff and also appealed for assistance from the French coast guard. Diana sailed out to sea to talk to a number of journalists on a press launch, to give a famous impromptu interview in which she claimed, 'You will have a big surprise coming soon, with the next thing I do.' This was widely interpreted to mean that she planned to leave Britain to live abroad, although a statement from her office at Kensington Palace the next day denied this and claimed that she had been misquoted.

For the young Princes, the holiday was probably everything they could have hoped. They loved the easygoing outdoor life, the jet-skis, and the yachts. Prince William was later to describe the magnificent yacht *Jonikal* as a 'fine piece of kit.' For the Princess it was much, much more. Although the massed press did not grasp the realities of the situation, hardly acknowledging the presence of Dodi Fayed, it was the beginning of a perfect romance, and the two were rarely apart.

Within a few days of the end of the holiday, Dodi whisked Diana away to Paris for a private weekend, staying in the luxurious Imperial Suite on the first floor of the Fayed-owned Paris Ritz. Returning on July 27, they left two days later for a six-day holiday on the *Jonikal*, cruising the Mediterranean off the French coast and heading south to Corsica and Sardinia. During the holiday they were joined by entertainers George Michael and Elton John, and rendezvoused with Mohammed Al Fayed's brothers, Salah and Ali Al Fayed, who were cruising at the time on the *Ramses*, another family yacht.

Everyone who encountered the couple during this happy period commented on how well-suited Diana and Dodi appeared to be. Their enjoyment of each other's company was almost palpable. They laughed and talked endlessly, their interests in music and films were the same, and they had no hesitation in displaying their intense happiness.

Diana had last found a man devoted to making her happy, while Dodi luxuriated in the company of the most famous woman in the world, who reciprocated his love so readily. The only thing which ever ruffled the Princess was the constant stream of gifts from the lovesick young Arab. She made it quite clear to her friends that he did not have to buy her love—it was there for the taking.

It was at this time that the world was first made aware of the romance. Tipped off by excellent contacts, fashion photographer and part-time paparazzo Mario Brenna tracked down the *Jonikal* and was offered no resistance to snapping away for several days. The pictures made Brenna a fortune, eventually selling for over £1.21 million ($2 million), and fuelling a feeding frenzy by the press of unprecedented proportions.

The couple returned to London on August 7, Dodi to his flat at 60 Park Lane and Diana to her home in Kensington Palace. The same night, Diana was photographed at the Park Lane apartment, not leaving until 11 P.M.

Almost immediately Diana had to set off for Bosnia for a charity mission with the Washington-based Landmines Survivors Network. While she was there, the Brenna pictures hit the street with the *Sunday Mirror* running eleven pages on the holiday and with a massively increased print run—once more the papers were in the money. At the same time other papers, angry at having missed the main story, started picking up on Dodi's past, investigating his business activities, his alleged debts, and his love life.

In Bosnia, the Princess fought a losing battle to keep the emphasis on the landmines issue as the press wanted to talk solely about her new romance. The day after Diana returned to London, the two of them boarded the Harrods helicopter for the short trip to the 500-acre Al Fayed estate at Oxted, Surrey, for a three-day break. It was during this holiday that the couple took the helicopter to visit Diana's clairvoyant, Rita Rogers, at her home near Chesterfield.

Back in London there were nights on the town and nights at the flat in fashionable Park Lane until Diana left London for a holiday around the Greek islands with her friend Rosa Monckton, president of Tiffany's in London, wife of Dominic Lawson (editor of the *Sunday Telegraph*), and daughter-in-law of Nigel Lawson. For once the Princess left the world's media in her wake, enjoying her holiday while the press combed the Mediterranean for her. Even so, a snapshot taken by a young vacationer on the island of Hydra still found its way into the *Daily Mirror* by the next day.

During this holiday Dodi was in Los Angeles trying to sort

out the Kelly Fisher problem, but he was back in London in time for Diana's return from Greece, and that same night the couple was again at Dodi's flat on Park Lane. It was now six weeks since the romance had started at St. Tropez, and on the following evening, August 21, the couple departed London for Nice and the final voyage on board the *Jonikal.*

Though destined to end in tragedy, it was another carefree break—an opportunity for Diana to put behind her the troubles of the past. For a few days she could free herself of the shackles she still felt bound her to the British Establishment, the Monarchy, and its menacing retinue of flunkies and advisors, the people she grew to believe were her enemies.

Chapter Two

Enemies Within

The world is full of cranks, so it is of little surprise that people as high-profile as Diana attract attention from snoopers and eavesdroppers. Many—indeed the vast majority—are harmless, and in the case of the Princess of Wales they could be coped with by those assigned to provide her with protection. The world in which royalty moves is mostly so distant from the general public that princes and princesses rarely come in contact with strangers except by appointment.

Those who might have had malicious intent and who occasionally represented a danger to Diana's peace and security were dealt with by a very active security team. What became known as the Squidgygate affair is therefore all the more curious, particularly in light of subsequent revelations, for it suggests that she might have had more to fear from the people appointed to protect the Royal Family than from the wider public. As is well known, this was her fear—that it would be they who would end up destroying her. As she mused, she would one day go up in a helicopter and never come down.

In the early 1990s, Diana was beset with leaks about her marital unhappiness. This was brought into focus when, in 1992, the *Sun* published extracts from an intimate conversation between Diana and James Gilbey, a car dealer, whom she had known since she was a teenager. There was little doubt that the conversation was genuine and Gilbey was obviously besotted with his friend. He referred to Diana as 'Squidgy' or 'Squidge' fourteen times and as 'darling' more than fifty times.

Whether Gilbey was more than a shoulder to cry on has never been revealed, but clearly neither would have imagined that their New Year's Eve chat, which included remarks about the problems Diana was having with Prince Charles and the Royal Family (and even about an episode of the TV soap *Eastenders*), would ever have been eavesdropped on. In fact, parts of the conversation were not only overheard by two amateur eavesdroppers, listening in on the same frequency band as James Gilbey's mobile phone, the conversation was also recorded by them.

Diana's conversation was wide-ranging and intimate. She felt she was becoming isolated within the Royal Family and expressed her worry at becoming pregnant. She was also worried about a meeting she had had with Gilbey being discovered. She said Charles made her life 'real torture': 'I'll go out and conquer the world—do my bit in the way I know how and leave him behind.'

About one Royal lunch she said: 'I nearly started blubbing. I just felt sad and empty and thought "bloody hell, after all I've done for this fucking family" ... it's just so desperate, always being innuendo, the fact that I'm going to do something dramatic because I can't stand the confines of this marriage.'

For Jane Norman, an Oxford-based typist, prying on other people's mobile phone calls was a hobby. She switched on her radio scanner and heard what appears to have been the beginning of the Diana/Gilbey conversation. Her recording ends with a few remarks that appear on the beginning of another a tape recorded by Cyril Reenan, a retired bank manager. Reenan appears to have recorded the remainder of the conversation, and he realized when it ended that it was worth big money. Within days he had approached the *Sun* newspaper, which waited for nearly two years before publishing the contents, until the relationship with Prince Charles had palpably broken down.

The Squidgygate tape was a sensation, but in many ways the circumstances of the way the recordings were made is even more interesting. It emerged from Norman and Reenan that the recordings were not made at the time of the call but four days later on January 4, 1990. If true, this could not have been due to a freak of nature, an ionospheric aberration. It meant that a third party must have recorded the conversation at the time it occurred, then played the tape later through a transmitter on the Cellnet frequency so that Norman and Reenan would pick it up.

Clearly dirty tricks were afoot, but who would do such a thing? Certainly money was not the motive. Would some amateur electronics nerd have gone to so much trouble simply to cause the Princess embarrassment? It seemed more likely that this was a more organized leak.

Further answers to the puzzle came out later when it emerged that a number of experts had investigated this breach of royal security. Audiotel International analyzed both tapes and concluded that though they were picked up by receivers tuned to the Cellnet frequency, they were not normal Cellnet signals. The data bursts on the tapes suggested 'some kind of doctoring,' the firm's report said. Pauses in the conversation were suspiciously lacking in interference and Andrew Martin, Audiotel managing director, concluded that they were unlikely to be the result of haphazard scanning. He added, 'The balance of probability suggests something irregular about the recording which may indicate a re-broadcasting of the conversation sometime after the conversation took place.'

These conclusions were supported by a study conducted by communications consultant John Nelson and audio expert Martin Colloms. They decided that the recordings could not have been made by intercepting the signals from a cellular phone base station. There was a fifty-hertz hum on the tape, suggesting there had been a tap on an ordinary telephone line. A spectrum analysis showed this was made up in places of two separate signals, indicating that a tape of the conversation had been subsequently remixed. The Princess' voice was of relatively poor quality for reception on the Cellnet band. More significantly, there were 'pips' or 'data bursts' on the recordings at eleven-second intervals. These would have been filtered out at the nearest telephone exchange prior to a Cellnet transmission.

Colloms and Nelson reported, 'We are forced to conclude these data bursts are not genuine but were added later to the tape. They originated with a locally made recording and show that an attempt has been made to disguise a local tap by making it appear it was recorded over cellular radio. The recording must have been made as a result of local tapping of the telephone line somewhere between the female party's telephone itself and the local exchange.'

Cellnet confirmed that its own internal investigation carried out in August 1992 came to precisely the same conclusion. Its spokesman William Ostrom said that the call was definitely not recorded off air but was an example of sophisticated eavesdropping. 'It is a very sensitive issue if a cellular network has been bugged,' he said. 'We wished to satisfy ourselves exactly what happened.'

Though these reports made few ripples and have never led

to a Government investigation, the conclusions are intriguing to say the least. There is no reason to doubt that Cyril Reenan and Jane Norman picked up what they thought was a Cellnet transmission, but the evidence shows that someone transmitted a fake Cellnet signal on the Cellnet frequency band, doctored to imitate a genuine transmission. Whoever did this had been able, four days earlier, to place a tap on Diana's direct line at Sandringham. And since the palace is equipped with its own exchange, the mystery eavesdropper must have had access to the palace premises.

The culprit (or more likely culprits) must have had access to sophisticated recording and editing equipment, including a special piece of equipment to transmit on Cellnet frequencies in the UHF band. It is clear that they were not motivated by money; they wanted people like Norman and Reenan to appear to be the eavesdroppers and gain any subsequent reward. This narrows down the people who might be responsible to palace staff and others with access to Sandringham estate. Thus it is hardly surprising that the security services are high on the list of suspects.

It is quite possible therefore that a group within these Government agencies were bent on discrediting Diana and causing her even greater distress and depression than the disintegration of her marriage was already generating. However, the plotting went further. Two weeks before the Squidgygate conversation another intercepted call was recorded, allegedly between Prince Charles and Camilla Parker-Bowles. The 'Camillagate Affair' broke in the newspapers in January 1990 and speculation about Diana's marriage reached its zenith.

This tape, the veracity of which has never been challenged by either party, was even more revealing—it dealt with intimate sexual matters. Charles apparently at one point talks about pushing the 'tit' of the telephone, and the woman friend replies, 'I wish you were pressing mine.' His response is, 'I love you, I adore you.'

According to Andrew Morton in his book *Diana—Her True Story,* now recognized as having been based on material from Diana herself, the Princess considered packing her bags and leaving at this point. Of the Squidgygate business she apparently said, 'It was done to harm me in a serious manner, and that was not the first time I'd experienced what it was like being outside the net so to speak, and not to be in the family.'

She seemed to be implying that some members of the Royal Family or their courtiers could be somehow behind the tapping of phones. Charles also had his suspicion of dirty tricks. According to the *Sunday Times,* he ordered a check for bugs in Kensington Palace by a private security firm because he could not trust Government experts. Such fears are of course extraordinary. That a future King of Great Britain and his wife could be bugged by servants of their own Government should be impossible. But as this book indicates later, it is folly to trust that officialdom will always play by the rules.

Almost from the moment his son Dodi died, Mohammed Al Fayed believed in the possibility that the British secret services could be responsible. As was well-publicized at the time, he told the *Daily Mirror* in early 1998 that he was 99.9 percent certain his son's death was not an accident. He told Thomas Sancton and Scott MacLeod, in their book *Death of a Princess,* how he could not get out of his mind that the British Establishment played some role: 'You can't believe what I am fighting here. They can't get over the fact that I own Harrods. It's an Egyptian not a Briton who built this store, this fantasy.... I won't stop until I bring down the rest of them. I won't stop until I reveal the true extent of the political conspiracy that I have been the victim of....'

It is fair to point out that the Harrods boss has long been consumed with anger at the way he was treated by the British Government in his battle with arch rival 'Tiny' Rowland, and at the way he was subsequently denied British citizenship. However, his suspicion about the crash in Paris led to the Harrods boss financing his own private investigation of the affair by his security chief, John MacNamara, while publicly placing his 'full trust' in the French probe headed by Hervé Stephan.

It was Al Fayed's much-publicized belief in a possible conspiracy theory, and his determination to discover the truth, that inspired what appears to have been a gigantic hoax. It was allegedly perpetrated by a group linked to the underworld and to various intelligence organizations, and headed by the intriguing figure of Oswald Le Winter, a sixty-seven-year-old American born in Austria. He came forward to make the sensational claim that MI6, aided by the CIA, was responsible for the crash.

The story began in late March 1998 when Le Winter, calling himself Oswald Lukas, contacted a prominent commercial lawyer in Beverly Hills, California, and claimed to have documents for sale proving a conspiracy by the British and US secret services to murder Dodi and Diana. The lawyer in turn contacted Mohammed Al Fayed, and his account of what was on offer must have been convincing, for it led to a number of meetings between Le Winter and MacNamara in the United States.

Papers were exchanged, although Le Winter refused to produce the crucial evidence until payment had been made — a figure said to be approaching £10 million ($16.5million). Le Winter was given an advance of £15,000 and the scene then moved to Vienna, the Austrian capital, for the final handover of the rest of the money.

Using the name George Mearah, Le Winter arrived there on April 20. The short, fat, bearded, and balding American checked in to the Hotel Stadt Bamberg, a two-star establishment close to the red light district. The booking was found to have been made by a former Czech agent with the rank of colonel, Karl Koecher. He was returned to the Soviet Union in 1985 in exchange for the release to Israel of a Jewish dissident, and is supposedly an accomplice of Le Winter's in the alleged Diana hoax. After Le Winter arrived in Vienna, MacNamara moved into the luxury Hotel Ambassador, and a meeting was agreed for Wednesday, April 22.

Unknown to Le Winter, he was already walking into a trap. Before MacNamara had set foot in Austria, Al Fayed had spoken to an old friend in the FBI who contacted the CIA. An elaborate plan was put into effect with Le Winter and his friends being spied on with listening devices and followed everywhere. It is said that agents for the FBI, the CIA, and possibly Mossad conducted a joint operation with the Austrian police, seen by some as overkill if it was all a hoax.

At the appointed time Le Winter, posing as George Mearah, arrived at the Ambassador Hotel and met MacNamara in the Lehar Bar. Further details of the deal were discussed and another meeting arranged for Friday, April 24. According to Austrian press reports, Le Winter at this point put a file of papers in front of the Harrods security chief, and then the Austrian surveillance team pounced.

As he was being dragged out of the hotel, Le Winter became hysterical. Some reports say that he was beaten up in the process. He screamed out that Al Fayed and MacNamara would pay for their treachery in the same way as Dodi and Diana. He shouted that he had five accomplices and one of them would take revenge on his behalf. Koecher was also said to have been picked up and—allegedly—roughed up.

Le Winter was taken before a magistrate and remanded in custody. It was found that he was carrying identity cards in false names purportedly issued by various American organizations. Stories appeared in Vienna that he was 'singing like a canary' about his dealings with Al Fayed's people.

The entire incident was mysteriously kept quiet for four days until the story was broken by one of Austria's top crime reporters, Peter Grolig, of the newspaper *Kurier.* It emerged that at the time of Le Winter's arrest, his hotel room was searched and a pile of documents discovered. Four of these, two of them in code, were found to be of crucial interest, as they seemed to be genuine CIA papers.

The motive for the alleged plot to kill Diana and Dodi was, according to these papers, of intense concern within the British Establishment. People were aghast that they might be planning to marry, with Dodi therefore becoming stepfather to a future King. Le Winter claimed Henri Paul had been poisoned and his Mercedes tampered with. His files were handed over to the Austrian Fraud Squad for checking, where the initial view was that they were fakes—'the best forgeries I've ever seen,' according to one source.

Faced with the story in *Kurier,* Harrods issued a statement confirming MacNamara's involvement in the sting. 'The case follows a two-week enquiry by Mr. MacNamara in Washington and Vienna into allegations that British Intelligence sought the help of the CIA in a plot to assassinate Diana, Princess of Wales and Dodi Fayed. Working with the full cooperation of the law enforcement authorities in the United States and Austria, Mr MacNamara was also investigating the alleged existence of documentary evidence of such a plot. There are no further details at present as enquiries are continuing in the United States and further charges are anticipated.'

Details about Le Winter now began to emerge. It transpired he is the son of a Columbia University professor and had been recruited to the CIA before turning renegade. In 1995, he was the key source for a TV documentary, partly financed by Tiny Rowland, which suggested CIA involvement in the downing of *PanAm 103* over Lockerbie.

Rodney Stich, author of a book about the CIA *(Disavow—A CIA Saga of Betrayal)* said that Le Winter worked for the agency for thirty years using the code named 'Razine' after being recruited during the Vietnam War while working as a college professor.

A TV reporter, Peter Koenig, recalled in the *Independent* on Sunday how he had spent some time with Le Winter in his home in the Mojave Desert, California, in 1996. He was trying to sell Koenig a document allegedly showing that Mark Thatcher, son of the former British Prime Minister, was involved in a drugs-for-arms deal with a Syrian businessman. Koenig could not verify the document and concluded he was the victim of a hoax, but he was intrigued by Le Winter: 'He constantly perspired. He was suffering, he said, from Epstein-Barr Syndrome, an immune deficiency disease. He spoke with a tough-guy New York accent. He championed the cause of Israel. Later, this advocacy metamorphosed into hints that he was an agent for Mossad. He was the best-informed person I have ever met on intelligence matters. His views on everything from geopolitics to literature were sophisticated.'

It emerged that Le Winter had spent a term in a German jail for smuggling amphetamines from Libya to the US, but claimed this was part of a mission for Colonel Oliver North, the man behind Irangate. Koenig believes he is a con man par excellence, one easily capable of initially hoodwinking an experienced former Scotland Yard police detective like MacNamara. The fact that the Harrods security chief paid Le Winter £15,000 before the sting was set up indicates that both his story and his initial documentation were highly plausible. But could it have had any grain of truth?

It is indeed surprising that as many as six secret service agents were involved in the arrest operation. People began to wonder if the official claims that Le Winter was selling forged documents might be part of an all-too-convenient cover-up by the security agencies themselves, who clearly could never admit to a Diana plot in which their own organizations had played a part.

The speculation increased when the Austrian Interior Ministry announced that papers found in Le Winter's possession had not yet been positively confirmed as forgeries. 'Their authenticity is still being examined,' said its press officer. It also emerged that a 'third man' was being sought, apparently an agent for Mossad. Like Karl Koecher, he had booked into the same hotel as Le Winter but disappeared before he could be caught. The CIA was forced to issue a denial. 'The assertion that the CIA played any role in the death of Princess Diana is ludicrous,' said spokesman Tom Crispell. Of course the CIA would hardly own up to such an allegation even if it was true.

If the suspicions discussed in this chapter are accurate, that some element with links to the British secret services exposed Diana's extramarital relations by tapping and re-broadcasting her phone calls, or a renegade group sought the help of the CIA in an assassination plot, how would anyone ever find out? The perpetrators would operate in the shadows, in a world where information is distributed only on a need-to-know basis.

The cardinal rule is: Make sure they are deniable. That is why the secret services periodically employ private detectives and professional crooks to carry out their dirty work. If any one chooses to blow the whistle, the public will be less inclined to believe their word against that of a respectable servant of the State.

This seems likely in the case of one infamous criminal, Peter Scott, born Peter Craig Gulston, who has disclosed that an attempt was made to recruit him for just such a purpose, the target being the Al Fayed family. He has disclosed to the authors that he was approached by people with impeccable links to high society who first wanted Mohammed Al Fayed killed, and later Dodi.

Scott has no firm evidence that later tragic events in Paris were part of a plot hatched by the people he met and who, he maintains, wanted him to arrange a hit. However, his story—if it can be believed—indicates that Dodi was in imminent danger from what Scott describes as 'the British Establishment' because of 'the Arab's' love for the Princess.

Furthermore, Scott did not keep what he had found to himself. He is adamant that he warned Hon. Frances Shand Kydd, Diana's mother, of a murder plot against Dodi three weeks before the crash in Paris.

Crooks are not normally noted for their honesty but Scott may well be a rare exception. His autobiography *Gentleman Thief,* published in 1995 by Bloomsbury, is an extraordinary catalogue of confessions about his life in the underworld. The book is a candid expose written with great fluency and packed with examples of his own failings.

It is a 'warts and all' account of one of Britain's most accomplished thieves, who was a brilliant cat burglar in his earlier criminal career when he was dubbed the Human Fly. It begins with a quotation by Gaetano Salvemini: 'We cannot be impartial, we can only be intellectually honest.... Impartiality is a dream and honesty a duty.'

Born in Belfast and educated well at the Royal Academy School, Scott had, by his own admission, conducted 150 burglaries before he was twenty. Now sixty-seven years of age, he is back in jail again. It is reckoned that over his extraordinary life of crime he removed £30 million worth of valuables—paintings, furs, and jewels—from the rich and famous including Elizabeth Taylor, Lauren Bacall, Zsa Zsa Gabor, John Aspinall, Sophia Loren, and Maria Callas. And, over the years, he spent or gambled away the entire fortune while serving a total of twelve years inside.

He said: 'I have an in-built suspicion I was sent by God to put back some of the wealth that the outrageously rich had taken from the rest of us.... I wasn't uncaring. I was generous to a fault. I suppose it was part of my Presbyterian upbringing to try to get a few plus points for being a persistent sinner....'

Beginning three years ago, Scott said he became aware that certain people 'including a former Tory Cabinet Minister' were eager to see Dodi's father, Mohammed Al Fayed, dead. He explained: 'There was a concrete offer doing the rounds here from the right sources to send Al Fayed home—dad, not Dodi. There was money on the table.... The Establishment were looking for a way to get rid of them.'

Scott said he had several meetings with a shadowy group linked to the British Establishment. The approach was oblique: 'Nobody asked me to do anything. Do you think those sort of people ask you to do anything? They have a discussion, they talk about everything.' As time passed Scott said he realized the group was alarmed by Mohammed Al Fayed's enthusiasm for cultivating people in high society, in particular Diana,

Princess of Wales.

Why was he approached by this group? According to Scott it was because he had known Frances Shand Kydd, Diana's mother, for more than forty years, a link that Shand Kydd has admitted. Recalling the early period of their relationship Scott said, 'She was a deb's delight and I was a rather handsome young robber baron. She didn't know what I did for a living.'

Scott said the group he was dealing with became more keen on securing his help when they realized he was still meeting Shand Kydd occasionally and corresponding with her. 'I write very strange good letters,' he said, 'and all I was trying to do all the time was to give her good advice about her happiness and her own life.' '[When they knew I was in touch] I became more useful.'

But was the group right to think Scott was capable of murder? He said his publisher cut out of his book a 'confession' that he had once killed a man in the Midlands who had tried to shoot him. The pair had fallen out over the theft of £100,000 ($165,000) worth of platinum. Scott said of his victim:, 'He was unlucky, not only did he not shoot me but he left the gun hanging out of his jacket pocket. When he was dragging me along to drop me in the canal I shot him dead and put him down the sluice.'

Scott explained that he was still resisting pressure to get involved with the group when, in early 1997, other events intervened. From the mid-1980s, he claims to have gone straight, earning a bit of pin money as a popular tennis coach in Regent's Park. However, in March 1997 he was tempted into crime once again, led into a trap by police who arrested him in the act of trying to sell a stolen Picasso painting, *Tête de Femme,* worth £650,000 ($1.07million). He had received the work of art from a notorious armed robber who had also been caught.

The one-time 'human fly' eventually appeared at Snaresbrook Crown Court, North East London, in May 1998, giving his address as Bemerton Estate, North Islington. At first he pleaded not guilty of conspiracy to handle the picture, alleging the police were acting as agents provocateurs. But as the jury was about to retire to consider its verdict, he suddenly changed his plea to guilty.

On leaving the court before sentencing he told reporters regretfully and in characteristically candid style, 'I was intellectually and morally convinced that after the prosecution's very skilful cross-examination, I could not continue to sustain this not guilty plea without jeopardizing ten years of honesty, decency, and hard work. I am a victim of circumstances.' He was given three and a half years.

The jury had heard that Scott had tried to sell the painting for £75,000 ($124,000) shortly after it had been stolen from the Lefevre Gallery in Mayfair in March 1997. The robber was Russell Grant-McVicar, thirty-three, who had produced a fake gun, taken the picture off the wall, and then made his getaway in a hijacked taxi. His comeuppance came at the Old Bailey a week after Scott was sentenced. Having been found guilty of sixteen charges of robbery, attempted robbery, firearms offenses, and escape (he had eluded prison guards while being held on remand in the hospital), the judge sentenced him to fifteen years.

Grant-McVicar is the son of John McVicar, now a journalist but who was once Britain's most-wanted man for his armed robberies, for which he received a twenty-six-year sentence. Father and son had been estranged for many years and John McVicar did not attend his son's trial. Scott, on the other hand, has known Grant-McVicar for a long time and is a surrogate father, even looking after him when he was on the run. According to Scott, attempts were apparently made to draw his friend into the threat against the lives of the Al Fayeds while the pair were both awaiting trial.

Two men from the group who wanted Al Fayed killed began to put more pressure on. At first, Scott said, 'The word was that if dad [Mohammed Al Fayed] gets ironed out, with a contract, one presumes that as he was the puppet master everything else would collapse.'

Then it was suggested that Dodi should be the target and that Grant-McVicar might make a suitable assassin. 'He [Grant-McVicar] didn't tell me about this. I told him. I said I think you can get yourself out of your current circumstances. There's a game plan afoot.'

Scott named the former Cabinet Minister who he believed was involved in the plan. 'He was in the plot. Have no doubt he was in the game plan.' He said he then wrote several letters to Shand Kydd, all before the death of Dodi and Diana, warning that the relationship between the two would soon 'end in blood red ruin.'

He added: 'I've been in the fast lane all my life. I know that sooner or later the wheel comes off. And I thought the perimeters of possibilities were going very narrow. She was getting photographed in skin-tight bathing suits with Arabs on the yacht. I thought she was off her rocker, or hell bent on self-destruction. My warning was that something nasty could happen....'

He was worried that someone else might intervene very soon. 'I said to Frances, a lot of people [want] to get rid of the Egyptian from the bazaar. I'm talking about Dodi. She has taken my letters somewhere. This isn't one of those phony prophesies after the event.'

Scott said he made no deal with the group he had been

meeting and as Grant-McVicar remained in jail no suspicion can be attached to him. He added: 'My gut instinct [about what happened in Paris], speaking from a lifetime in the business, is that it wasn't what it seems. Somebody stuck something under the Mercedes and that car in front, the missing car, was able at a distance to push a button, and probably blew one of the tires.

'I've known senior people in the underworld, and the general word is that it wasn't an accident. There was a story in Paris that the Israelis were involved in a tit-for-tat operation in return for concessions.'

Scott said that Shand Kydd never replied to his messages and instead he received a letter from her Edinburgh solicitors telling him to break off contact. Then on the morning of the Paris car crash she rang. He said, 'When Diana died, I imagine I was the first person she phoned, very early. It doesn't matter what she said. I wrote her a letter with a poem by A.E. Housman.' Scott's story is disturbing and intriguing, but is it true? He spoke only reluctantly about his meetings with the group who wanted the Al Fayeds targeted, and about his letters to Frances Shand Kydd. Also, he sought no payment for the interview and expressed annoyance at the idea that, as he suspected, the content of his letters to Shand Kydd had been leaked.

He also said he was saddened that no one apparently paid any attention to his letters, although he suspects the police saw them. At the very least, his testimony shows that one should not take for granted that Diana's death was simply a dreadful case of drunk driving. At most, it indicates that there was indeed a plot to murder Diana and Dodi, that the orders came from the top, and that only an investigation in Britain will solve the riddle.

Chapter Three

Pillar of Faith?

Love and celebrity have been both friends and enemies to the Al Fayed family of Alexandria, Egypt. Mohammed Al Fayed, and his son and heir Dodi, have both known fame on a global level—a level which would have been unthinkable even a few generations ago. While Mohammed actively sought out this recognition and must have clearly welcomed it, Dodi had an even greater fame thrust upon him. For both, it proved an acquaintance most people would probably rather not encounter.

In life, Dodi's relationship with the Princess of Wales brought him instant fame on an unimaginable scale, which not even a life of exorbitant wealth and luxury could have taught him to handle. However, it is possible to speculate that, in death, he may be remembered as little more than a footnote to history.

Until mid-summer 1997, it was the father Mohammed who was the better known of the two. While Dodi was dabbling in films in Hollywood and establishing his 'playboy' status, Mohammed was courting publicity as the controversial businessman and owner of Harrods, the London department store.

His fame edged towards notoriety during his extensive battles with 'Tiny' Rowland, chairman and chief executive of

Lonrho, who charged Al Fayed with irregularities during the acquisition of the Harrods company. At the same time, his failed attempts to gain British citizenship also brought unwelcome publicity, as did the British 'cash for questions' scandal, which not only brought opprobrium on the heads of several Conservative MPs (including Neil Hamilton) but arguably contributed to the collapse of the Tory Party in the 1997 election.

Dodi's early years hardly prepared him for a life of fame. His mother deserted the family home when he was just two years old, and for the following six years he had virtually no contact with her. These years are generally considered to be a crucial time in a child's development, and this desertion was to affect his self-confidence and self-esteem for the rest of his life. Family, friends, and acquaintances all remember him as an awkwardly shy and diffident child who did not mix easily.

On April 15, 1956, Dodi was born to Mohammed Al Fayed and his first wife Samira Khashoggi, who at nineteen was barely out of school. They lived in Alexandria, Egypt, and in contrast to his fabulous wealth today (he is generally considered to be a billionaire), Mohammed Al Fayed's early years could be described as no more than comfortably middle class. Mohammed's father was a schoolteacher and there was little in the way of inherited wealth.

Samira Khashoggi's background was altogether more exotic; she came from a very wealthy family in Mecca and her father, Dr. Mohammed Khashoggi, was the royal physician to King Saud, the founder of modern Saudi Arabia. Samira had two sisters and three brothers; the boys, Adnan (later to become a notorious arms dealer, dubbed the richest man in the world), Essam, and Adil, were sent to Victoria College, a boarding school in Alexandria, the Arab world's equivalent to Eton.

Dr. Khashoggi was a sophisticated man with unusually liberated views and opinions within the Arab world. He decided that his daughters should also be sent away for a first-class education. Samira and her sister Assia were enrolled in the English School in Alexandria and, with all the children now based in the City, a house was acquired in Alexandria so that their mother could be close by while Dr. Khashoggi remained in Mecca.

The Khashoggis had another child while the mother was in Alexandria, a second sister for Samira. It was at this time that Mohammed Al Fayed and Dr. Khashoggi became friendly and, as the association matured into trust, he eventually offered Al Fayed, already a skilled and ambitious trader, a position managing a new import/export business in which he had an interest. The company prospered and eventually provided the springboard for Mohammed Al Fayed's later remarkable success.

The links between the families became closer as the business association prospered, and the ties moved from the purely commercial to the point where the families were meeting socially, and it was on the fashionable Alexandria beach that Mohammed Al Fayed met Samira Khashoggi. They married and set up home in a modest house near the rambling property of the Khashoggi clan.

Their first, and indeed only, child arrived quickly and the doe-eyed boy was christened Emad El Din (Arabic for 'pillar of faith') Mohammed Fayed. When just a toddler and learning to speak he had difficulty with all the *D*s in his name and as he stuttered over them his family quickly nicknamed him 'Dodi'.

Happiness for the young family did not last long. When Dodi was barely two years old, Samira announced that she no longer loved Mohammed and was leaving him. In truth, she had fallen in love with her cousin Anas Yaseen, who was a business partner of one of her brothers.

Mohammed Al Fayed was deeply hurt, and as a result he cut virtually all ties with Samira. He gained custody of young Dodi, patriarchal custody being quite a common practice in Egypt in the event of a divorce, although in a stable family environment babies usually stay with their mothers until around the age of eight. Dodi hardly saw his mother for the next six years and, with his ambitious father building his career, Dodi's upbringing was left largely to nannies and relatives.

For Samira, life seemed blissfully happy with her new husband, Anas, who was a rising star in the Saudi diplomatic service. Living first in Beirut, the couple was soon moving between countries frequently as her husband was appointed ambassador to India, the United Nations, and then Turkey. Once again, however, her happiness was not to last—in 1974, Anas was killed in a road accident in Turkey, leaving Samira devastated and alone.

Being an educated and intelligent young woman, she could not and would not settle for a life of wealthy ennui, so she embarked on her own entrepreneurial career. Her first venture was to establish the Arab world's first magazine for women, called *El Sharkiah* (The Oriental). A number of romantic novels followed, two of which were turned into film scripts for successful Egyptian films. Samira married yet again, this time to a Lebanese businessman, but sadly, the marriage did not last. Her third husband left her for another woman, and in 1986, lonely, sad, and full of guilt for leaving her only son in infancy, Samira died of a massive heart attack.

Meanwhile, in Alexandria, the upwardly mobile Mohammed had purchased a large house in a fashionable part of the city. Dodi's aunt, and uncle Salah, moved into this house and became largely responsible for supervising Dodi's education.

Because of his disjointed upbringing, with his mother gone and his father chasing dreams of business and financial success in many countries around the Middle East, Dodi matured into a shy and diffident person, never quite sure of himself or of others' reactions to him. Many people around him found this difficult to understand, as he appeared to be the boy who wanted for nothing. He was given his first car on his thirteenth birthday, and although he crashed it on the very same day, there were to be other cars, as well as yachts, in the beautiful bay of Alexandria.

Dodi's education was also the very best money could buy— in his early years he was enrolled in the exclusive College St. Marc in Alexandria, where the French monks ran a strict and perhaps even harsh regime. Along with other children of the rich and famous he too was subjected to discipline which would barely be tolerated in the relatively liberal atmosphere of British schools. A quick cuff round the ear (which would land any British school teacher in the courtroom) was regarded as a normal daily occurrence. In addition to this, parents would be called in at the drop of a hat if it was felt that pupils were not putting in their best effort.

Dodi's father or Uncle Salah probably dreaded calls from the school, as it is clear that the young Dodi was by no means an academic star. In fact, it is a matter of record that when he left the College he was marked thirtieth out of the thirty-eight pupils in his year.

At the tender age of thirteen, he was dispatched to Switzerland. It may well have been a sound educational decision, but to Dodi it must have seemed harsh. As a youngster suffering the first pangs of puberty, being sent away may well have compounded his feelings of rejection and represented a further abandonment. The school he attended was the famous Institut Le Rosary at Rolle, close to the jet-set ski resort of Gstaad and coincidentally not far from the finishing school Diana was to attend just a few years later.

It would seem that the young Dodi did not appreciate the regime at Le Rosary, for he left just one year later without either graduating or completing his course. However, his time at the Institut was far from wasted, for it was during this period that he met many of the people he would remain friends with throughout his life, especially some of the children of the Hollywood film set.

It was this group who helped influence his later decision to become involved in the movie business. But what Dodi did for the next few years is something of a mystery. When he was sixteen he returned to the United Arab Emirates for military training. In common with most of the sons of the business and political elite in the Middle East, this was simply the precursor to a spell at Sandhurst, the Royal Military Academy in Berkshire, Britain. Here Dodi completed his six-month course and was duly commissioned Second Lieutenant in the U.A.E. army before joining the Emirates' Embassy in London as a junior attaché.

In this capacity he would have had little power, but some influence, in a region where arms dealing is a billion-dollar business. He became even closer to his uncle, Adnan Khashoggi, notorious as the biggest dealer in the game. As the flamboyant Khashoggi was prone to quoting, 'If one offers money to a government to influence it, that is corruption. But if someone receives money for services rendered afterwards that is commission.' And his commissions were bigger than some countries' GDP.

It was during this period that the foundations for Dodi's

reputation for loving life to the full, as did his uncle, were being laid. He was remembered by his old friends in Alexandria as being a timid lad, despite his early displays of great wealth, who often needed help in finding a girlfriend. No doubt these friends were quite surprised to hear that Dodi was becoming a jet-setter. A lifelong admirer of *Playboy* magazine, Dodi subscribed fully to its free-living philosophy and with the financial backing and support of his father he could live out that dream in full.

School friends remember him in this period as being physically well endowed and adopting a love-them-and-leave-them attitude to his girlfriends. He appeared reluctant to make commitments and was fearful of rejection, a likely result of his mother's abrupt departure when he was a child.

From his teens onwards, Dodi had access to classy apartments, houses, or mansions in all the top locations around the world. There was a flat in Park Lane, widely recognized as London's best address, houses in New York, Dubai, and Milan, a chalet in Gstaad, as well as the Fayed-owned estates and mansions in Scotland and Berkshire. Shortly before his death, Dodi bought a beautiful beach-side house in southern California.

Then there were his cars: there would be a fleet waiting wherever his private jet or Sikorski helicopter landed. During the 1970s and 1980s Dodi took the London nightclub scene by storm. As he roamed the capital's hottest clubs he would be followed by two chauffeured cars, a white Rolls-Royce, and a red Ferrari Testarossa. Which of these cars he used to return home in was determined by the girl he picked up.

The young Dodi was also particularly proud at that time of the Mustang which he had imported from America, and in front of which he enjoyed posing as a hippy. There was also a Mini Cooper with darkened windows, and a specially converted US military jeep.

With so many luxurious accoutrements at his disposal it is hardly surprising that Dodi attracted the opposite sex in droves. Among the women with whom he associated were many from the world of film and show biz, including Valerie Perrine, Mimi Rogers, Tina Sinatra, Ali McGraw, Britt Ekland, Winona Ryder, Charlotte Lewis, Patsy Kensit, Joanne Whalley, Lynsey de Paul, and Cathy Lee Crosby. It is a list of which Hugh Hefner (the legendary founder of *Playboy*) could well have been jealous.

Many of the ladies in his life retained fond memories of Dodi. Marie Helvin described him as 'simply a nice, lovely, always friendly man and always really generous.' He was 'madly in love' with Brooke Shields, with whom he spent some time in Gstaad. He later sent her a large bunch of roses when she married André Agassi.

Dodi discovered Koo Stark when she was filming *Electric Dreams* and spent time with her in Los Angeles. Later, he was very proud of his girlfriend Julia Roberts, introducing her to his father and looking after her during her London appearances.

Catwalk models were equally attracted to Dodi, and many famous names from the world of fashion adorned his arm. Among them were Marie Helvin, Amy Brown, and Kelly Fisher, his last love before Diana. He dated Julia Tholstrup, and also Suzanne Gregard, whom he met when she was featured in his film *F/X—Murder by Illusion*. They later married in the winter sports town of Aspen, Colorado.

A few of his girlfriends were a little derisory of his prowess in bed and complained of his lack of affection. 'There was nothing tactile about Dodi,' one complained, adding, 'he was not inclined to linger after love-making, there were no cuddles or caressing and kissing.' Despite this he was always generous—gifts of jewelry, flowers, holidays, and all the toys the wealthy have at their disposal were all part of his courtship.

Gregard was his wife for just ten months, but she remembers him with great affection for his kindness, consideration, and for his lack of arrogance. This is a recurring theme from those who knew him well, from the staff he interviewed for jobs, to the people who served him in restaurants, and those on his personal staff. Almost without exception they recall a polite and respectful person, soft-spoken, a ready smile, always immaculately dressed. Perhaps this is why he rarely made it into the gossip columns, despite his wealth and amours.

From Dodi's mid-thirties onwards, his father wanted him to become more involved in the family businesses, especially in the management of Harrods and the Ritz in Paris. The pressure would have been difficult to resist, for Mohammed Al Fayed suffered none of his son's reticence. In fact he was a dominant and controlling influence throughout his son's life.

Dodi became a director of Harrods, where he was involved with product development and public relations, introducing Hollywood stars to host special in-store events and to open the annual January sales. At the Ritz in Paris, the president Frank Klein remembers Dodi as a friendly colleague who would introduce ideas or suggestions for changes without pressure. 'There were no orders with Dodi,' said Klein, 'he would simply present his arguments for change with reasonable discussion and without raised voices. He was a pleasure to deal with.'

Despite all these moves into commerce, Dodi's first and last love was the movie business, in which he achieved considerable success. His friendship in London during his mid-teens with the producer Cubby Broccoli's daughter Barbara first lit the fires of his interest. She took him on visits to the sets where her father's James Bond films were being made, and introduced him to many of the actors and technicians.

This schoolboy obsession intensified when he attended the cinema summer school in New Orleans with Cubby's son Tony Broccoli. And it was to be the connections with the Broccoli family which eventually launched his career. Anxious to help the young Dodi on his way without getting bitten by the many sharks patrolling the movie industry in Hollywood, Broccoli advised him to link up with established Hollywood filmmakers.

Dodi formed Allied Stars Ltd. in mid-1979 when he was just twenty-three years old with a Broccoli associate in the driving seat and his father providing the cash. Although often an absentee director, Dodi was full of enthusiasm and ideas. Jonathan Pryce starred in *Breaking Glass,* the young company's first venture, which was an immediate success, covering its costs and making several million dollars profit. The film is still shown in art cinemas around the world.

This was quickly followed by *Chariots of Fire,* which went on to be nominated for seven Oscars and brought Dodi instant recognition as a serious player in the movie world: as executive director he won the coveted Academy Award for Best Motion Picture. He celebrated in true playboy fashion by spending a riotous summer on the Côte d'Azur. Fast boats, fast cars, and a jet-set lifestyle were the order of the day for the budding film tsar and his many friends.

His career in the industry was to last for around fifteen years, during which time he produced films on his own account, such as his two F/X movies, one of which ironically told the story of a fake government assassination. In 1991 he was the executive producer of the Peter Pan–inspired story

Hook, starring Robin Williams, Julia Roberts, and Dustin Hoffman, and directed by Stephen Spielberg.

His final involvement in the movie industry came in 1995 with *The Scarlet Letter,* directed by Roland Joffe and with Demi Moore playing the role of Hester Pryne. Tinsel Town insiders recall that Mohammed Al Fayed was behind every film involving Dodi, who was rarely allowed to make a decision on his own. 'Everything had to be cleared through Mohammed Al Fayed. Nothing happened without his approval.'

If this was frustrating for Dodi he did not show it, but it was a very real example of how the dominating Mohammed controlled most aspects of his son's life. Despite this parental control and a distinctly part-time approach to the industry, Dodi certainly achieved his youthful ambition of becoming a recognized player in the industry.

The end of Dodi's movie career came not because of a lack of ideas and certainly not because of a lack of money, although a parental reluctance to loosen control of the purse strings could have been a factor. Ever since childhood friends remember he rarely had cash in his pocket (even though he had ready access to money). They say Dodi demonstrated a 'relaxed' attitude to settling accounts and regularly left them to pay for their outings.

Financial matters came to head in the mid-1990s when a string of actions against him appeared in the California courts for failure to pay bills. Many related to the rental or lease of luxury apartments in and around Los Angeles, while others concerned credit-card transactions where Dodi claimed the goods did not meet his expectations.

No doubt his expectations were high. Yet more complaints emanated from business associates who claimed that Dodi owed them money, and there was also conflict with the Internal Revenue Service. At this stage in their careers, of course, Mohammed Al Fayed was more widely known in international circles than Dodi and, as the stories of the court actions appeared in leading international newspapers, Mohammed was fearful that the bad publicity would reflect on his carefully nurtured reputation.

There was certainly something of a rift between the two at this stage, with Dodi fretting at his lack of self-determination in the organization of his life, and Mohammed wanting Dodi closer on hand to control his excesses and to prevent the 'playboy' tag from reflecting on the business empire he had so carefully developed. Mohammed was constantly having to fend off critical comments about his links with various British MPs and the allegation that his money had not come from his own endeavors but from the Sultan of Brunei.

By the end of 1996, Mohammed had all but given up hope of becoming a British citizen or of curbing the taunts leveled at him in Britain, but he is still a proud man and a fighter. He penned a heartfelt letter to the *Times* expressing his frustrations and his contempt for his enemies: 'Many hard things have been said about me, but it is cruel beyond measure to imply that I am seeking acceptance by "the Establishment." I am not seeking acceptance by any self-perpetuating caste, I only wish to share the nationality of my four British children.

'I do not wish to receive honors or titles, I never go to fashionable restaurants, and I cannot remember the last time I attended a reception or society gathering that was not directly connected with my commercial concerns. My interests are my family, my companies, and my staff. I serve all my customers well—not just those who consider themselves to be the Establishment.

'I have never kept the receipts of any journalist visiting

L'Hotel Ritz in Paris; nor did I put up the £7.8 million ($12.8 million) to keep Canova's statue The Three Graces in this country, though I offered to do so if no one else would foot the bill. I did not make a donation to the Hampton Court restoration fund, though I have admired the completed work and was pleased to present a promotion in my store on behalf of the Royal School of Needlework which is housed in the palace.

'I am proud of my Egyptian origins, but I love this country, even if that is unfashionable. Without wishing to boast, I should point out that my estate in Scotland is 50,000 acres, not 30,000; I recently enlarged it, not least in order that I might get even further away from the goings-on of some of the MPs who make up a decaying "Establishment" I would never join.'

The letter summed up his fury at being thwarted. All the money in the world could not buy him and his family acceptance in his adopted country. Mohammed was frustrated with Britain and frustrated with his son, confiding to friends of Dodi's that he was wasting away his life.

A jet-setter; a playboy; a Hollywood film-maker; heir to one of the world's wealthiest men; whatever title is given to Dodi Fayed there appears to be one word which is commonly linked to them all, and that is 'drugs.' There were never any police allegations or charges of substance abuse against Dodi, and it is unlikely that drugs ever played a dominant role in his life. But it is equally unlikely that drugs were totally absent.

In the sophisticated, affluent world in which he circulated, whether on the West Coast of America, in the Swiss mountains, or in the clublands of London, drugs were part of the common currency. It is no secret that Dodi had a distinct weakness for models, and dated many of the most famous girls from the butterfly world of high fashion. Many make no secret of their liking for drugs, and it certainly can be no coincidence that the gaunt heroin look was high fashion during the summer of 1997.

To be with such exquisite creatures and not join them in such a little weakness could well have been seen as a touch on the wimpy side. Drugs have always been easily available to the super-rich, and while Dodi has not been the subject of police investigations, the same cannot be said of other members of both his extended and close clan. His favorite uncle Salah Fayed was the subject of intensive police interest during a trip to Scotland in June 1993.

Drugs have a minor role in the investigations by the French authorities into the crash at the Place de L'Alma. It has been emphasized from the start that no drugs were found in the possession of any of the occupants of the mangled Mercedes. Nevertheless, reports exist that police took hair samples from Dodi, Henri Paul, Trevor Rees-Jones, and the Princess, and it would be strange indeed if toxicological examinations have not taken place.

Also there have been allegations that Henri Paul, Assistant Director of Security at the Paris Ritz, had a close personal relationship with Dodi Fayed, and may well have been a principle supplier of drugs. This, it has been suggested, could account for some of the vast sums of money deposited in Henri Paul's bank account shortly before his death, and also for the wad of cash found in his pocket at the crash scene.

Many friends have testified over the years that Dodi was generous with drugs. They do not say he was a big customer, but that he was a regular customer, and very often he bought them as much for his friends as for himself. It was part of the self-doubt in Dodi's nature, a sense of inadequacy compared to the fabulous success of the father on whom he was dependent for money and favors, that Dodi had a need to impress people with his kindness and generosity.

It is a theme stressed over and over again by friends and acquaintances. One informant interviewed after the crash said that 'he was a member of the jet-set drug scene,' while another opinion was that he had 'more than one contact with cocaine.' This was confirmed by an ex-girlfriend, Nona Summers, who reported that 'he snuffed cocaine but had such problems with it that he gave it up.'

This same lady also told a story about a meal shared in a New York restaurant favored by the Fayeds, where the star guest was film actor Jack Nicholson. 'Dodi placed an enormous, almost priceless white truffle in the center of the table. While the guests were messing about with it, it almost fell off the table—and they all laughed,' said Miss Summers.

In a report which appeared in *Vanity Fair* magazine, a friend of Dodi's recalled an evening in a suite in the Waldorf Tower Hotel in New York. 'That was the only time in my life that I saw a kilo of cocaine. It was in Dodi's apartments. It was his week's ration for his friends and himself. I was there as it made the rounds and the cocaine heads disappeared into the bedrooms.'

The suggestion that Dodi bought the gear for others as much as for himself was supported by Jack Martin, a Hollywood insider, who apparently spent months at Dodi's expense staying at the luxurious New York Pierre Hotel where the Fayed's kept an apartment. 'He was a wonderful man,' said Martin, 'who bought far more [drugs] for others than for himself. That was his generous nature. He loved to buy it, to give and to share.' And it has been widely reported that life on Dodi's yacht *Sakora* was all 'sex, drugs, and rock'n'roll.' It was on the *Sakora* that Paula Yates spent wild nights with INXS singer Michael Hutchence, not long before he died in what was widely reported to be a drugs-driven suicide.

As mentioned above, there have been no drugs allegations against Mohammed Al Fayed, but the same cannot be said for his youngest brother, Salah, who was involved in a very strange episode on a trip to the Fayed's Castle at Balnagowan in Ross-shire, north of Inverness, reported first in the *Scotsman* newspaper.

The story, according to the paper, started when Salah took a trip to Balnagowan Castle from London in the company of a young female trainee manager on the staff of Harrods. They missed their flight to Inverness and took an alternative flight to Aberdeen, many miles from their destination. Without missing a beat, Salah hired a local taxi to complete the journey. On his way home the taxi driver stopped in Elgin to make a telephone call and, climbing back into the car, discovered a large leather handbag left on the back seat.

Wondering what to do, not wanting to drive all the way back to Balnagowan, he took a quick look in the bag and discovered what was to him vast amounts of money in dollars, sterling, and Swiss francs, along with a number of Polaroid pictures and some correspondence.

'Too hot to handle,' he thought, and handed it in to the Elgin police station. The officers on duty made a more extensive search and discovered a small amount of a 'grey white substance' which the officer thought could be crack cocaine, along with a number of pills and a worn homemade pipe and pipe cleaner.

In the paper's words, 'The discovery started a flurry of phone calls, involving Mohammed Al Fayed himself, and later Sir David McNee, former chief constable of Strathclyde and former Commissioner of the "Metropolitan Police" who was an advisor on security to Al Fayed and Harrods. The owner of the bag was said to be the young lady "trainee" accompanying

Salah Fayed on his trip to romantic Scotland, who showed, however, absolutely no expertise in setting up the pipe for use and for whom the money in the bag would have represented many years of salary.'

These events took place in June 1993. The Crown office said, 'We can confirm that.... Grampian police submitted a report to the Procurator Fiscal's office in Aberdeen in relation to a woman and property found in a taxi which was hired at Aberdeen airport. No proceedings were taken.'

It would be wrong to tar Dodi with the brush of suspicion, but it is clear he moved in a world where drug-taking was common.

He was not a 'pillar of faith' as his name states, but this charming and unassuming man should nevertheless have had few direct enemies. Could Dodi have become such a threat to the British ruling elite as to warrant planning his death, as Peter Scott alleges? If so, why?

In truth, he was a foreigner. He was the son of a business-man who had bought his way into British society and who helped bring down a Government by exposing wrongdoing—his own. He was the relative and friend of Adnan Khashoggi, the biggest arms dealer in the world. He was planning to marry a future King's mother. In some people's minds this would be enough to make him a target of the Establishment his father so thoroughly despised.

Chapter Four

Final Hours

For Diana and Dodi, Saturday, August 31, 1997 had been an unsettling day. It had started incredibly well; Dodi was ecstatically happy, busy planning the most momentous event of his life. After the wonderful Mediterranean holiday, Dodi was now running some important words through his head—just how do you propose to a Princess who is the most famous woman in the world? That night, he intended to formally invite the Princess to become his wife. And he had every reason to anticipate a joyful acceptance.

Diana was still floating on a cloud of happiness after the 'bliss, absolute bliss' of their holiday and was keenly anticipating a reunion with her adored children the following day. Perhaps she had an inkling of what Dodi was planning for the evening, and perhaps she was thinking, rehearsing, the words she would use if her answer was yes and she had to break the extraordinary news to her two sons.

Their plans had been really quite simple; after all, when you have the resources of such a vastly wealthy family at your disposal, everything can be made simple. The Paris trip was only intended to be for a single night, with the first port of call the magnificent house on the Bois de Boulogne, formerly home to the Duke and Duchess of Windsor and now leased by

Mohammed Al Fayed from the French Government.

Dodi had already confided to Frank Klein, director of the Paris Ritz, who was also responsible for all the Al Fayed interests in France, that he planned to marry the Princess and that this was the home in which they would settle down. Just a few weeks earlier, Mohammed Al Fayed had announced there would be an international auction of all the contents, some 40,000 items, at a glamorous sale in New York. It is now widely seen as a necessary preliminary before Dodi and his Princess bride could move in.

Following their visit, they would then drive to Dodi's magnificent ten-room apartment off the Avenue des Champs-Elysées in rue Arsène-Houssaye to relax and refresh themselves after the rigors of their journey from Sardinia. Then there would be a shopping trip for the second major objective of the Paris visit. Before Dodi could ask the Princess the most important question of his life, he had to collect the £125,000 ($200,000) 'Tell Me Yes!' *(Dis-Moi Oui!)* ring. It had been chosen by the couple at Alberto Repossi's discreet jewelers in the Hermitage Hotel in Monte Carlo on August 22.

During their Mediterranean cruise, Dodi had directed the *Jonikal* to Monaco for the specific purpose of choosing a ring from his favorite jeweller. A little over two weeks earlier, on August 5, the couple had looked at rings in the exclusive boutique and carried off a catalog.

On the second visit they had a very clear idea of what they wanted: a stunning ring of yellow and white gold with diamond clusters in triangle formation enclosing a dramatic emerald. However, it was not quite what she wanted and jeweler Repossi promised to make the desired adjustments and deliver the ring personally to his shop close to the Paris Ritz for collection on August 30.

For Diana and Dodi, the day started at a leisurely pace. All the arrangements for their journey to Paris had been organized and confirmed by the worldwide team of executives, security experts, and secretariat of the Al Fayed empire. The couple had woken quite late and enjoyed an informal breakfast on the deck of the *Jonikal* anchored off Sardinia's Emerald Coast.

The weather was perfect, with the morning sunshine shimmering across the rippling waters. Just before midday Dodi's butler, René Delorm, transported the luggage across to the little quay at the back of the hotel Calla di Volpe. Shortly afterwards, the couple boarded the *Jonikal*'s launch for the short trip ashore to the waiting taxi, which would take them to Olbia airport where the Harrods' green and gold Gulfstream IV jet would whisk the couple off to Paris.

Also on board were Dodi's masseuse, on constant duty because of a back problem, a housekeeper, and two bodyguards. The journey took a little less than two hours and the sleek private jet touched down at Le Bourget airport, some ten miles (16Km) to the north of Paris, a little before 3.30 P.M.

Although there had been no paparazzi on the journey from the *Jonikal* to Olbia airport, the situation was about to change dramatically. News of their arrival in Paris had clearly been leaked to the press. Whether the information came from the London tabloids, the most prolific source of information for the picture-hungry pack, or from somewhere else in the world, it was quite clear that their hopes of a quiet romantic stopover in Paris were totally destroyed.

Dodi could see the pack of photographers quite clearly from the aircraft, and he was furious. He was livid because he knew that Diana felt truly hunted by the paparazzi and also because he had believed that the vast resources of the Fayeds could protect her.

His reaction to them could well have clouded his judgment; at this moment, a number of decisions were taken which may have contributed in some way to their deaths just a few hours later. All the resources of the French Service de Protection des Hautes Personnalités (the SPHP) were available to the couple, due to Diana's position as a former member of the British Royal family and mother of the heir to the British throne.

There are conflicting reports concerning the role of the SPHP. One says that the select force were not officially notified of the couple's arrival. Another says that they were aware of the arrival of the Harrods jet, that they knew who was on board, and that they made several offers of assistance.

The SPHP is a trained force, well-used to dealing with the problems of moving foreign dignitaries around the French capital safely and discreetly, and the French authorities would certainly have wanted Diana to use this powerful and fully resourced service. It is known that the SPHP, from their headquarters at Roissy airport, spoke directly with the pilot of the Harrods Gulfstream IV. The offer was clearly made to provide protection during their stay in Paris and, in particular, provide freedom from the paparazzi.

Dodi, it is said, refused their assistance. As the sleek jet taxied to the Transair terminal, where Paris Ritz VIP arrivals are traditionally looked after, an SPHP car pulled up beside the aircraft. Again, the offer was put forward of a special security car with dark tinted windows. Dodi chose once more not to avail himself and the Princess of this service.

In fact, it has been reported that the offer was made a third and even a fourth time when the party's cortege reached the Paris Ritz. While the hotel manager, Franc Mora, was greeting them in the grand foyer, an officer of the SPHP appeared yet again. 'The car is waiting outside and we recommend that you use our service,' he explained.

Despite further rejection, the officer persisted. 'If you will not use our car, we recommend that two police cars accompany you on your excursions around the City.' But Dodi was not to be shifted. 'We want to spend the last hours before we part in private and intimate surroundings,' Dodi is reported to have told the SPHP officer and the managers at the Ritz. Perhaps he truly wanted to live up to what he saw as his role— protector.

In retrospect, there were probably a number of conflicting reasons for Dodi's rejection of the service's help. Although he was often described as a quiet, considerate, and charming person by many of his closest friends, there was another side to the man's character. As Dodi's long-term live-in lover Kelly Fisher testified, he could be arrogant, self-centered, and demanding when dealing with hotel staff.

It is quite possible he believed that the security offered by the hotel was, or should be, equal to that of the SPHP. Perhaps he was anxious to impress the Princess that the resources of the Fayed family were more than sufficient to provide her with all the security she needed. He also knew that Diana was deeply suspicious of official security staff. Her position entitled her to twenty-four-hour-a-day protection by the Royal Protection Squad, quite apart from the relentless attention of MI6.

Throughout the fraught years of her conflict with Prince Charles and the British Royal Family, Diana had often felt betrayed by them, believing that they not only monitored her every move but listened in on private telephone conversations and reported everything back to Palace officials. As we have seen, she also believed, probably quite justifiably, that some of the most lurid stories about her private life which found their way into the tabloid newspapers came directly from the British security services with the tacit approval of the Royal Family.

She believed that this was how the story of her fling with Captain James Gilbey had become national headlines. Knowing all this it is possible to understand that just hours before he was planning to propose to the Princess, Dodi wanted to impress her with the all-encompassing security of the Fayed empire. No outside assistance was needed.

Even if it is possible to find a way through the maze of complex thoughts in Dodi's head, it is still difficult to understand the constant refusal of assistance from the SPHP which was simply a protected travel service. The results, of course, were tragic.

At the airport, the paparazzi were parading at the Transair terminal, among them many of the photographers who would feature in the events of the night, including Chassery, Oderkerken, and Romauld Rat together with his motorcycle driver Stephane Darmon. As the passengers, led by Trevor Rees-Jones and followed by the Princess of Wales, disembarked the aircraft the cameras recorded every move.

After the Princess came another bodyguard, Kes Wingfield, followed by Dodi and finally the masseuse and housekeeper. Greeting them on the tarmac was Henri Paul of the Paris Ritz, well known to both the Princess and to Dodi. Photographs show a particularly warm welcome from Diana and a conversation with Dodi, possibly explaining the plans for escorting the couple into the center of Paris.

There could well have been other things to discuss, like the money which was later discovered, unaccounted for, in the security man's bank account and on his person. It is one of the mysteries of the crash that Paul had so much cash.

There were two cars waiting for the party: a super-luxury, black Mercedes 600 with tinted windows, owned and driven by Philippe Dourneau and under permanent contract to Dodi to chauffeur him when he was in Paris. There was also Dodi's personal black Range Rover, driven by Paul, acting head of security at the Paris Ritz. He was not normally used as a driver by either the hotel or Dodi. The Princess and her lover went in the Mercedes with bodyguard Rees-Jones, while Kes Wingfield, the masseuse, the housekeeper, and the butler traveled with Henri Paul.

From the outset, the plan was for the couple to go first to the Windsor house on the Bois de Boulogne, then on to the jewelers and M. Repossi. Dodi's grand flat in the Avenue des Champs Elysées area was where they were to rest before going out to dinner, and it was where they later intended to spend the night.

Harassment by the paparazzi from the moment the vehicles left the airfield perimeter was an early sign that these plans were likely to be blown off course. By the time they reached the A1 motorway, the cars and motorcycles of the paparazzi were buzzing all around them.

Diana was reported to have been both terrified of them and frightened for their safety. Witnesses from other vehicles on the A1 that afternoon confirm that the photographers were all around the two-car convoy, with one in front actually attempting to slow down their progress along the motorway, and with the flashes from the cameras reflecting in the windows of the two cars.

Even so, in an echo of what may have been tried later, some skillful driving by Philippe Dourneau enabled the Mercedes to shake off the pursuing pack as the cars came closer to the center of Paris and he was able to deliver the couple to the Windsor villa on schedule without too much trouble.

Meanwhile, the Range Rover carried on to Dodi's apartment with all the luggage and the rest of the party. As arranged, Henri Paul then reconnected with the main party in the Bois de Boulogne.

The couple spent no more than forty minutes touring the very grand building, with five acres of ground in the wealthiest part of Paris. It would have seemed a house of dreams for Diana and Dodi, taking him one step closer to the royal world after which he and his father so much aspired.

To Diana it must have represented a delicious step in the other direction, away from the bonds of royalty and into the world of those other great escapees and royal pariahs, the late Duke and Duchess of York—Edward and Mrs. Simpson.

Next stop for the miniconvoy was the Ritz Hotel, where they arrived soon after 4.30 P.M. Already the paparazzi and other inquisitives were gathering. The couple was welcomed at the luxurious entrance on the Place Vendôme by Claude Roulet, assistant to Frank Klein, the Fayeds' top man in France, after which they headed straight for the hotel's most luxurious apartment, the $10,250 (56,000ff)-a-night Imperial Suite on the first floor.

It was from here that the Princess telephoned London journalist Richard Kay, whom she regarded as both a friend and a confidant. In the next day's *Daily Mail,* Kay reported, 'She told me she had decided to radically change her life. She was going to complete her obligations to her charities, to the anti-personnel landmines cause, and then, around November, would completely withdraw from her formal public life.'

He also wrote, 'On that Saturday evening, Diana was as happy as I have ever known her. For the first time in years, all was well with her world.' To his colleagues, Kay reported that Diana was in love with Dodi and, equally importantly, she believed that he was in love with her and believed in her.

During the same conversation, Diana told Kay that she was puzzled why the British press was so hostile towards her Egyptian boyfriend. Even though Diana was a 'woman of the world,' she could be strangely naive—almost unworldly.

She appeared to think that the hostility might arise from the fact that he was a 'millionaire,' although she might just as easily have said 'billionaire.' The truth is, however, that everyone expected her boyfriends to be wealthy. What they did not expect, of course, was that her boyfriend might be a divorced Muslim playboy who had enjoyed relationships with an extraordinary number of the world's most famous actresses, models, and other sundry celebrities.

While Diana slipped downstairs to the hairdressers by the Ritz swimming pool and leisure complex, Dodi took the opportunity to make arrangements to collect the engagement ring from Repossi. In keeping with his prudent way of going about these affairs, he first sent Claude Roulet and Kes Wingfield across to the discreet jewelry boutique just a few hundred yards from the hotel. Satisfied that everything was in order, he was then driven across to the shop where he collected it, plus another which he maybe thought Diana would like to consider.

The second ring was returned. For a couple of hours there was peace for those scurrying around the VIPs. The lovers relaxed in the luxury of their suite, while the ever-attentive Claude Roulet made a discreet dinner booking for five at the fashionable Chez Benoît restaurant in the rue St. Martin near the Georges Pompidou Center.

Enjoying the prestige of a Michelin Star rating, the Chez Benoît was a favorite of Diana's but it was hardly to be a romantic occasion. The Paris press reported that the other three chairs around the table were to be occupied by two Frenchmen and an Arab who would be financing a planned branch of the Fashion Café for Paris.

If Diana was thinking of getting involved in the Fashion Café, it would have represented a considerable coup for Naomi Campbell, Claudia Schiffer, and Elle Macpherson, the three supermodels who front the worldwide chain of restaurants, including branches in New York and London. But it would seem out of character that on the night Dodi intended to get engaged, they should be discussing the launch of a theme hamburger restaurant.

In any event, the meeting was never to take place. Diana and Dodi jilted their three dinner companions, fearing, it is said, the attentions of photographers in a restaurant with a conspicuous picture window.

Dodi also spoke on the telephone that afternoon to his maternal step-uncle, Hassaan Yaseen, a Saudi businessman who was staying at the Ritz that weekend, and invited him to join them for coffee at the Chez Benoît around midnight, after they had finished the planned dinner. Another relative, his half-sister Jumana, was also in Paris that weekend and they planned to meet with her on Sunday to celebrate her thirty-second birthday.

Perhaps Dodi was anxious to tell his family his good news and good fortune as quickly as possible, but those were two meetings which sadly never took place. As a final detail, Dodi telephoned his butler at the apartment where they were to spend the night and instructed him to make sure to have champagne on ice ready for their return that night.

With the arrangements for the rest of the day all in place, Dodi and Diana were ready to leave the Ritz by 7 P.M. and, remembering how successful the ploy had been on their previous trip to Paris on July 25–27, they decided that they would leave by the rear exit of the Ritz on the rue Cambon.

Once more they climbed into the Mercedes 600 chauffeured by Phillipe Dourneau and set off, followed by the Range Rover with Trevor Rees-Jones and Kes Wingfield on board, now driven by Jean-Francis Musa, boss of the Étoile Limousine company.

They made their escape from the hotel relatively easily, but all this changed when they arrived at Dodi's luxurious apartment on the rue Arsène-Houssaye, not far from Les Champs Elysées and close to the Arc de Triomphe. As the little convoy pulled up outside the apartment, all hell broke loose. The paparazzi had been staking out the street, and swiftly surrounded the vehicles as they came to a halt.

It was the typical photographer frenzy which Diana had come to dread, and this time she felt seriously under threat. Romauld Rat, six-foot-plus (1.8m) tall and solidly built, who had been waiting at the airport and who had tailed the party on the A1 into Paris, was there as usual. With the paparazzi shouting, arguing among themselves and forcing their way too close, it was a scuffle to get the couple inside the entrance.

It was widely reported that the paparazzi were frighteningly abusive and, as the couple was attempting to get from the car to the door, there were many menacing remarks. Rat was shouting his protest at a Ritz security man who had put his hand over the lens of his camera, while yet another was threatening to call in the British paparazzi, who had an even worse reputation. Yet another was swearing to trash the name of the Fayeds: 'We'll tell everyone they're scum!' he yelled.

Inside the apartment, the Princess was shocked at the growing ferocity of the photographers. Despite all her past clashes with the paparazzi, this experience had left her bewildered and shaken, pale and frightened. Romuald Rat, in particular, had appeared to be a menacing figure and although described as a gentle person by colleagues in the Gamma agency, his sheer bulk and attitude had obviously affected Diana in the scuffle.

Dodi was pale for a different reason. He was white with anger. He lacked Diana's experience in the harsh media world and found it even more difficult to handle. It is possible that he also felt humiliated by the failure of the Fayed security team to protect the Princess from the assault, especially after rejecting the assistance of the SPHP and the Royal Protection Squad. Anger and humiliation are a dangerous cocktail of emotions, and the evidence suggests it was to affect every decision taken during the rest of the day.

For two hours, the shaken couple were able to relax and recover in the splendor of the second-floor apartment overlooking Les Champs Elysées. While Canadian butler René Delorm cosseted them, Claude Roulet was checking arrangements for the evening. With Frank Klein, the President of the Paris Ritz, away on holiday in Antibes, his assistant Roulet was determined to uphold the reputation of the Ritz for perfection. Nothing must go wrong on such an important night, especially while he was in charge.

By 9 P.M. he was hovering outside the Restaurant Chez Benoît, determined to see the couple safely to their table and their Fashion Café meeting. By 9.30 P.M. the couple was ready to go, the Princess casually dressed in long white Versace leggings and a white Versace blazer with a dark shirt. Her jewelry included a golden Jaeger Le Coulte watch, a Tiffany's bracelet, a gold ring with white stones, and gold earrings.

Dodi was also casually turned out in blue Calvin Klein jeans, light brown cowboy boots, and a Daniel Hechter wild leather shirt. His jewelry included a Cartier watch, a Breitling watch with no band, a broken Citizen watch, a leather cigar-case, and a metal band engraved with 'ID. Fayed, blood group B positive.' In his pocket was a golden cigar-clipper from Asprey, the royal jewelers in London, which had been a present from the Princess.

As the two-car cavalcade moved off, the media circus started all over again. Within seconds the Mercedes and Range Rover were surrounded by the paparazzi's motor bikes and cars, the reflections of the camera flash guns bouncing off the vehicle's darkened windows like terrorist weapons. Once again, the couple found themselves in terrifying conditions and all of Dodi's earlier anger came boiling explosively back.

It became increasingly apparent that the behavior of the photo-snappers was going to make it impossible for them to keep the dinner appointment at Chez Benoît. With a quick change of plan he ordered the harassed chauffeur, Philippe Dourneau, to head instead for the Ritz while he canceled the dinner date on his mobile phone.

A few moments later, the vehicles pulled up outside the Ritz, where Dodi was disgusted to discover the same madness going on. If anything it was even worse, for in addition to the photographers the crowd was boosted by tourists and general gawkers until there were maybe a hundred or more crowded around the entrance.

There were also several people picked up on the hotel's security videos who appeared to have been there most of the day and were still watching events, quietly from the edge of the crowd. They did not appear to be either press photographers or casual onlookers. Their identity has never been satisfactorily explained.

On their arrival at the hotel, Dodi was furious with both his bodyguards, Trevor Rees-Jones and Kes Wingfield, for not telephoning ahead to let the hotel know they were coming, until they pointed out that they were only following the car and at that point hadn't a clue what was going on.

The arrival of the cavalcade at the hotel caused chaos among the staff. Roulet, standing outside Chez Benoît, realized what was happening and called the hotel, but by the time his call got through the couple had already arrived. So much for his careful plans that nothing should go wrong.

As Diana climbed anxiously from the car, Kes Wingfield had to use all his power and experience to keep the photographers from jamming their cameras in her face. Witnesses were appalled by the way the Princess was treated and were frightened for her safety. It was a fear she obviously shared. Despite all her years' experience with the paparazzi problem, she had never experienced anything as frightening and ferocious as this.

But of course, the stakes had never been so high. It was common knowledge in the world of the freelance photo agencies that the newspapers were now prepared to pay extraordinary money for a good picture, especially if it took the story of the romance that little bit further. Up to a quarter of a million pounds ($410,000) had been earned just days before for a single picture of the couple kissing, and the French photographers were anxious to get their fingers into such a golden pot.

The big money on offer was turning these natural hunters into ruthless predators, prepared to fight anyone for the enormous rewards. As Diana was rushed through the crowd into the hotel, Dodi continued to sit in the car, his face a grimace of rage. This was not the evening he had planned.

Eventually he forced his way through the throng and into the hotel where he found Diana slumped in a chair. It was all becoming too much. According to onlookers, she looked crushed and defeated.

Trying to impose some order onto their evening, they arranged to be escorted to the hotel's grand restaurant, L'Espadon. Not even this proved successful. The wealthy Ritz patrons, globe-trotting jet-setters, and the Paris elite proved no more sophisticated than the gawkers outside. Their unwelcome attentions became equally unbearable to the couple and they decided to move themselves and their dinner to the privacy of the Imperial Suite, where they had spent several hours during the afternoon.

It was to be another two hours before they would venture outside the Ritz for their final horrific journey. Each part of the jigsaw was in place. The couple was trapped inside the hotel. The paparazzi, the curious, and several unidentified men waited outside. Most would have felt that their day's work was nearly over and that soon they could get some rest. Perhaps there were some who knew that this was not how things would work out.

One of the prime reasons for this speculation is the theory that Diana was already pregnant. Rumors were circulating in London and elsewhere for some weeks prior to the crash. It was a lively topic of conversation and debate at dinner parties, but until the crash the speculation was contained within certain sections of society, particularly those elements which liked to think of themselves as sophisticated and on the fringes of the court, and also among certain elements of the press.

Newspaper offices are traditionally hotbeds of rumor, and stories circulate rapidly in the rarefied atmosphere of the London-based nationals. As a topic of conversation it provided a delicious and slightly salacious element of scandal and gossip, but never built sufficiently to become a story strong enough to warrant any public speculation in the columns of the press.

Not even the tabloids, ever desperate for Diana stories, shared this exciting tidbit with their readers, although Diana's comment to journalist Richard Kay that she would be ready to step back from her public duties in November 1997 was widely regarded as a strong indicator of pregnancy. By that time it would be impossible to hide her physical signs.

The story was also linked to Diana's offshore chat with journalists during the holiday with the Al Fayed family in St. Tropez, when she told them that the next thing that she did would be a 'big surprise,' although in truth she and Dodi were only just getting together at that time and it is unlikely that she would have known if she was pregnant (by Dodi at least).

A more likely explanation for that particular comment is that she had plans to live abroad, a move which she felt would be approved by her young sons who had been upset by her treatment by the British tabloids.

Rumors of a pregnancy had also developed in the gossipy avenues of Alexandria and elsewhere in the Muslim Middle East, where the romance of the beautiful British Princess and the young Egyptian heir was followed with intensity and pride.

However, the polite and rather cultured nature of the rumors changed dramatically following Diana's death. As news of the disaster spread through the world, the pregnancy stories swirled into prominence and, led by the Egyptian press, became a central theme in explaining the deaths.

It is, of course, a straightforward and simple argument. The birth of an Anglo-Arab child to the internationally famous couple was seen as a matter of great pride for the Egyptians, bringing prestige to their country and raising it in the estimation of the rest of the world. As a concomitant of this it was accepted that such a birth would be fiercely resented by Israel, for there is an argument that anything seen as favorable for the Arabs is inevitably against the interests of the Jewish nation.

It was also readily accepted that the birth of such a baby would be seriously resented by the Establishment and even among the great mass of the population in Britain. The problems which such a birth would cause constitutionally to the Monarchy became a subject discussed with great intensity in the Middle East's newspapers and became immediately central to the surge of assassination and conspiracy theories.

So far the question of whether or not the Princess was pregnant has not been satisfactorily answered and will remain a hotly debated secret unless and until the French and British authorities publish unexpurgated details of medical and accident reports. That these authorities know the truth cannot be doubted, but at the moment every enquiry is met with a stonewall 'no comment' rather than a denial.

It is said that a British television company acquired evidence, never broadcast, that when in London before her second trip to the Mediterranean, Diana visited a Harley Street clinic for a scan which showed she was pregnant. Notwithstanding these stories, the truth of a pregnancy would have emerged during the many tests carried out by surgeons fighting to save the Princess' life in the Pitié-Salpêtrière Hospital in Paris. Blood tests would have been carried out as a normal procedure, and a test for pregnancy would have been likely for it could affect the nature of any treatment.

It is also extremely likely that the doctors would have carried out an ultrasound test as part of their life-saving efforts. This is the same procedure experienced by most pregnant women to check for a safe and satisfactory pregnancy. The baby's image can clearly be seen on a screen and can be printed as a 'photograph' showing the fetus in the womb. The details of all these tests would be attached to the medical file.

In their book *Death of a Princess* Thomas Sancton and Scott MacLeod report a number of medical rumors which they were unable to verify. One concerned reports of a confidential letter from Dr. Pierre Coriat, head of anaesthesiology at Pitié-Salpêtrière Hospital who tended to the Princess on the night of her death, addressed to Jean-Pierre Chevenement, the French Minister of the Interior, stating that Diana was nine to ten weeks pregnant.

They claim that a photocopy of the letter circulated around the editorial offices of several French newspapers but was never published after it was declared a fake by both the doctor and the Minister. They also report that a doctor at the crash scene in the tunnel suggested that the Princess was pregnant. This doctor allegedly told a colleague that Diana had rubbed her tummy and told him that she was six weeks pregnant.

Again, there has been no proof of this incident and there is also considerable doubt whether the Princess spoke at all after the crash. A further story related in *Death of a Princess* concerns a 'respected French journalist' who told the authors he had been told by a physician in the team working on the Princess that a blood test was taken and that it proved she was pregnant.

When this doctor looked at Diana's medical records several days later, 'all the test results had been removed.'

Once again it proved impossible to verify the accuracy of this story, and it remains another plank in the construction of conspiracy theories. All medical reports would normally be passed onto the police investigation team to become part of their report, but it has been reported by French sources close to this team that the French pathologist Dr. Dominique Lecomte did not carry out an autopsy and as a result of 'instructions received,' no blood samples were taken during what was little more than a cursory examination of the body.

An inquiry to the French coroners office about the possibility of pregnancy was also met with the response, 'No comment. That is part of the investigation.' It seemed almost calculated to add to the speculation.

The French authorities were forced into a response when a Spanish magazine *Interviu,* on December 29, 1997, published the alleged letter from Dr. Coriat to Jean-Pierre Chevenement saying the blood tests had revealed 'a state of pregnancy of nine to ten weeks.' The letter was denounced as a fraud by a spokesman for the Pitié-Salpêtrière Hospital, who surprisingly confirmed no tests were taken in this regard. The role of the doctors, they said, was to save Diana's life, nothing else. As Sancton and MacLeod point out, if the answer was this simple, why did they not give it earlier?

A further opportunity to reveal the truth will come at the full-scale public inquest into the death of the Princess to be held in Britain by the Royal Coroner, Dr. John Burton, after the results of the French inquiry have been published. Information on the question of a pregnancy will certainly be available at that inquest, but as Dr. Burton has the authority to hold the inquiry in camera it is likely that the curtains will again be drawn on this sensitive subject.

The authorities, particularly in France, are withholding information under the all-enveloping screen of medical secrecy and confidentiality. They could also be acting at the request of the Royal Family and the British Government on the basis that such information would be deeply wounding to Prince William and Prince Harry.

Nevertheless, concealment of the truth will do nothing to dampen the widespread belief that the Princess was pregnant at the time of her death, and will continue to add fuel to the fires of conspiracy theories.

Chapter Five

Steps to Disaster

Climbing wearily into his black Austin Mini parked outside the Champmesle bar in rue Chabanais, Henri Paul reflected on a difficult day. He had been battling with intrusive press photographers since the moment his boss, Dodi Fayed, had flown into Paris earlier in the afternoon, and now it looked as though it was going to start all over again.

Moments earlier, Paul had received a troubling call on his mobile from François Tendil, night security manager at the Paris Ritz. Tendil was a worried man. He was faced with the unexpected return of the owner's son, who was clearly in a fury, and there was no one to turn to for help.

The chief executive of the Ritz, Frank Klein, was still on a holiday in Antibes, and Claude Roulet, the number two, was stranded on the pavement outside the Chez Benoît restaurant where Dodi and the Princess had been expected to dine that evening. Although Paul had never been appointed to the top security post at the Ritz, he had been acting head since Jean Hocquet had resigned just over a year earlier. His confident manner and close relationship with Dodi made him the natural man for Tendil to call.

Paul would have learned that Dodi had again been hounded by the press, was back in the hotel, and was not happy. So shouting a goodbye to the women in the Champmesle, a largely lesbian establishment, Paul pointed his little car in the direction of the Hotel Ritz.

Evidence which became available later from the CCTV cameras showed he had a problem parking by the back entrance of the hotel in the Rue Cambon. Although there was plenty of space, Paul went into a complicated set of maneuvers before the little car was parked to his satisfaction.

It has been suggested that this was an early sign that he had been on a drinking spree since he had finished work around 7 P.M. that evening after the safe delivery of Dodi and Diana to the flat near Les Champs Elysées. But parking is bumper to bumper in the streets around the hotel and there was probably a space for nothing bigger than a mini at this time of day.

Paul enjoyed his work and took his responsibilities seriously, but to the best of his knowledge there was nothing else on his schedule for the day, and there was no reason why he should not have been relaxing with a drink. It was also completely natural and instinctive that he should decide to return to the hotel once the call from Tendil came through. If there was likely to be a problem he would want to be in the thick of things. Sadly, it was a decision which was to have a terrible consequence.

Among the many mysteries still surrounding Henri Paul is how he had spent the time between 7 and 10 P.M. on August 30, 1997. Did he put back several shots of some liquor because he was secretly a long-term chronic alcoholic as some people allege? Or was he no more than a moderate, selective drinker as testified by his family and friends?

His blood alcohol level after his death, measured variously at 1.74 g/l and 1.87 g/l, compared to the legal limit of 0.5 g/l, points to a monstrous drinking spree. However, to achieve such a high blood alcohol level in just a few hours, it would be necessary to drink at least half a bottle of liquor. It is of course possible that he had been drinking earlier in the day, and there is some evidence of this, even though it would have been out of character when he was on duty.

Independent evidence exists which confirms that he had been drinking quite heavily on the day before the crash, including in the restaurant Armand-Palais-Royal with a blond girlfriend, who may have broken up with him that day. Reports also say that he was drinking on the Saturday of the crash.

In the morning he enjoyed a drink with his friend Claude Garrec after tennis at the club at Issy-les Moulineaux, and then later at the Brasserie du Pelican in the rue Croix des Petits-Champs. By all accounts, the evidence to suggest that Paul had been drinking that day is tenuous.

The owners and staff of the bars in central Paris where he was in the habit of popping in for an occasional drink all claimed that they either had not seen him that evening or that he had been drinking lightly.

There is an alternative possibility that he had been drinking alone in his apartment, and a number of empty and partly consumed bottles were discovered there. This, of course, is far from conclusive evidence for they may not have been touched that day.

Blood tests after the crash discovered traces of the prescription drugs Prozac and Tiapridal. The former can make one feel uninhibited and the latter can reduce reaction times and affect eyesight. Taken together with alcohol they could cause a slight personality change, turning an introvert into an extrovert, but medical opinion is that it might have made him a better driver.

Even back at the hotel there were conflicting reports of his condition. Off the record, a number of junior staff were to tell reporters that Paul was a well-known drunk and there was video evidence that he spent part of his time at the hotel that evening with bodyguards Trevor Rees-Jones and Kes Wingfield at the Vendôme Bar. But both denied that he had been drinking in the hotel.

When it was pointed out that on the video he is seen drinking a 'yellow liquid,' they promptly said they thought it was pineapple juice which he had diluted with water because he found it too 'strong.' It has since been established that the yellow drink was, in fact, pastis, a favorite with the French who dilute the aniseed-based aperitif with five parts water.

According to the photographers 'door-stepping' the main entrance to the hotel, many of whom knew Henri Paul well, he was acting out of character that night. Henri went out front a number of times before midnight to talk to the press gang. Normally he was a somewhat dour character, but on that night he was animated—almost playful—joking with the photographers and telling them that they would not have to wait long for some action.

By 11.30 P.M. the crowd outside the hotel had grown to around a hundred gawkers, including approximately thirty photographers and paparazzi. The two vehicles used throughout the day, the Mercedes 600 and the equally elegant Range Rover, were parked ready for the couple at the front of the hotel. But the size of the crowd and the troubles with the press since they arrived in Paris that afternoon were enough to make Dodi think another plan would be necessary.

In the back of his mind he knew that the rear entrance to the hotel in the rue Cambon was used frequently by guests wishing to make a quiet exit; he and Diana had used it themselves in July during their secret visit to the French capital.

At about 11.30 P.M., it is claimed, he telephoned his father, Mohammed Al Fayed, back at his estate in Oxted, Surrey to discuss a new plan of action. What he had in mind was to use the cars at the front of the hotel as a decoy while another vehicle quietly collected himself and the Princess at the back door.

According to the reports, Mohammed Al Fayed did not agree with this at all. He wanted the couple to stay in the Imperial Suite. It offered all the luxury that money could provide and would avoid any further clashes with the paparazzi.

Dodi, it seems, was determined to return to his private apartment on the somewhat slim pretext that that was where their belongings and luggage were, waiting for their departure the next day. Everyone prefers to have their own things around them, but this seems an unlikely reason to leave the hotel. After all, there were a dozen members of staff who would fetch their bags at the click of a finger. Yet it appears that the lure of more personal surroundings was stronger than the fears of harassment on the journey.

There can be no doubt that the attentions of the photographers had caused Dodi and the Princess severe stress during the events of the day. The anger in Dodi's face can be seen quite clearly in the CCTV video footage. Yet the question has to be asked whether there was just possibly a frisson of excitement in it too. It is common knowledge that Diana positively enjoyed having her photograph taken, especially when she could be in control of the situation.

Is it also the case that Dodi was beginning to respond to the excitement, even the perceived glamour, of all the attention? Whatever the reason, the die was cast; Dodi was determined to go through with his plan. Another car would be needed and another driver.

There were a number of vehicles available on the premises belonging to International Limousine, a competitor of Étoile Limousine, who owned the car in which Dodi and Diana died. International kept a fleet of more than a dozen vehicles at the Ritz.

For one reason or another, International's cars and drivers were overlooked. This meant that only vehicles owned by Étoile Limousine came into the reckoning, and the only car they had available that night was another Mercedes, not a top-of-the-range 600 series like the one parked at the front, but a model S-280. This was luxurious, but lighter, somewhat less powerful, and without the protective dark-tinted windows.

It also had a checkered history. Earlier that year the car, which was kept at the Ritz for the exclusive use of its guests, was stolen in mysterious circumstances. On duty for the hotel, the car was parked outside the exclusive Taillevent restaurant on the rue Lamennais waiting for guests to finish their meal. Without warning, the driver's door was flung open and the chauffeur dragged from the vehicle by three Arabic-speaking men wielding handguns.

'It was like a commando attack,' the driver said later. The vehicle disappeared for nearly two weeks before turning up in Montreuil in a distressed condition. The wheels were gone, the door had been ripped off, the complete electronic system and the box controlling the ABS braking system had been stolen.

The Mercedes France dealer in Saint-Quen where the vehicle went for repairs costing 15,000 Francs($2,750) reported it was the work of professionals. If this is true, it raises the following question: did they simply steal from the vehicle, or did they take the opportunity to plant something menacing on it?

If they did, the target would have been the Fayeds, or maybe one of their celebrity guests, for at that time Dodi and the Princess were not a recognized couple. As far as anyone is aware, their romance started certainly no earlier than June, although Mohammed Al Fayed may have dreamed of the notion far earlier.

Having decided on his plan of action, Dodi required an additional driver. There were a number available, including Jean-Francois Musa, proprietor of Étoile Limousine, and Philippe Dourneau, who had been driving the bigger Mercedes for the couple all day, and those chauffeurs working for International Limousine.

Although a smaller vehicle, the Mercedes waiting at the back door of the Ritz was registered with the Paris police as a 'grande remise' vehicle requiring a properly licensed driver to be at the wheel. Both Musa and Dourneau held this special police license. Henri Paul, who was chosen to drive almost certainly by Dodi himself, did not.

The moment he got behind the wheel he was technically breaking the law, although he had been trained by Mercedes on similar vehicles. So why was Paul chosen? With the benefit of hindsight it would have been logical for him to drive the Range Rover, and for Musa or Dourneau to drive the small Mercedes. That Dodi decided differently, if indeed it was him, may reflect the special relationship he enjoyed with Henri.

There were many pointers to this special relationship. There was the animated and warm greeting earlier in the day when Paul met the couple at the airport, and the equally animated discussion seen on the security video as the party was waiting in the corridor of the Ritz to leave on the last dreadful journey.

While there is no suggestion that Paul overstepped the employee/employer relationship, he was certainly more than a mere servant. Reports circulating in the French and German press suggest that Paul was Dodi's guide and mentor to the demi-monde of Paris life. It is said that Paul knew his way around the sex-and-drugs world of the capital and had built up wide connections servicing the wealthy and famous when their needs were outside the law.

It has been claimed by a famous Paris fashion photographer that Paul provided Versace models with cocaine. It has also been alleged in the French/German press that he was Dodi's guide to the houses of 'sin' in Paris and also a principal supplier of drugs. This would help explain a number of things, including the 300,000 Francs(54,900) deposited in Henri Paul's bank account shortly before the day of the crash, and the fact that he had 20,000 Francs(3,660) in cash on him when he died.

By midnight on August 31, 1997, the plan was formulated and the vehicles and their drivers in place. At the front of the hotel was the Range Rover to be driven by Jean-François Musa, with Kes Wingfield in the passenger seat, and the Mercedes 600 to be driven by Philippe Dourneau.

These were to leave with the maximum of noise and fuss, distracting the crowd from the events taking place at the rear of the hotel where Dodi and the Princess would leave with Henri Paul driving and Trevor Rees-Jones in the passenger seat. Later both Wingfield and Rees-Jones claimed that the plan did not have their approval.

They felt there should be a back-up car with the couple and that both the bodyguards should be with them. Dodi was said to have over-ruled the idea of both the security men going along as the 'Mercedes was too small.' That may well have been true, but there would certainly have been room in a second car, and there were plenty available.

What must not be overlooked is that the journey from the Place Vendôme to Dodi's apartment off Les Champs Elysées is little more than a quarter of a mile, and even after the experiences earlier in the day, perhaps he felt that employing four cars to get them home was a touch too elaborate.

Already the plan to make a quiet exit from the rear of the Ritz was coming apart at the seams. Experienced Paris photographers were aware that the ruse had been used before and several were waiting along the rue Cambon, keeping in touch with their colleagues at the front of the hotel by mobile phone.

Soon after 12:15 A.M., as Dodi and the Princess were making their way from the Imperial Suite overlooking the Place Vendôme on the first floor of the Ritz to the rear door, the Mercedes S-280 was driven from the garage for Henri Paul to take them home. Paul knew the photographers were there; they later reported that he was waving and signaling to them.

So much for Dodi's big plan. With Henri Paul and Trevor Rees-Jones already on the pavement, Diana emerged from the hotel first, closely followed by Dodi, and the car pulled briskly away at 12:20 A.M. Kes Wingfield took a phone call to say the party was leaving, and he gave instructions for the Range Rover and the 600 series Mercedes to make a flashy departure from the front of the hotel. A few followed them but already the paparazzi at the rear of the hotel were calling their colleagues at the front on their mobiles to tell them what was happening.

The two-car decoy convoy left the Place Vendôme by the rue de Castiglione, turned right onto the rue de Rivoli, and traversed a quarter of the Place de la Concorde before swinging right onto Les Champs Elysées. Finding the road busy, they turned left at the rond-point down the Avenue F. D. Roosevelt before joining the Seine expressway joining at the Cours Albert 1er.

At this point they unknowingly joined the route of the

smaller Mercedes. As they arrived at the Place de l'Alma there were already signs of a commotion as they swung right up the Avenue George V to the Arc de Triomphe and Dodi's apartment.

During the journey they received a surprising telephone call from René Delorm, Dodi's butler, asking if he had time to walk the dogs before the couple arrived. 'They should be with you already,' said the bodyguard Wingfield, who then tried to ring his colleague Rees-Jones to find out where they were and what was happening. It was a call which never made contact.

Paul pulled briskly away from the rear of the Ritz down the rue Cambon, turning right onto the rue de Rivoli where he was caught by a red traffic light at the rue Royale. By this time the paparazzi were buzzing up behind the car. Obviously aware that just a couple of hundred yards from the hotel the whole plan had gone disastrously wrong, Paul accelerated away moments before the lights changed, surging left around the Place de la Concorde and then right onto the Seine express-way at the Cours la Reine.

What he planned, it would seem, was to drive along this route, normally reasonably clear at this time of the night, until reaching the Chaillot Palace at the Place de Trocadero from where there are a number of alternative routes back to the apartment off Les Champs Elysées. On the Cours la Reine Paul could see a long straight road ahead of him for nearly 600 meters, and he urged the car violently forward away from the pursuing paparazzi.

The road swings down into a tunnel under the Pont Alexan-dre and the Pont des Invalides before rising to the surface again on the Cours Albert 1er at the end of the straight. A left turn takes the road down into the tunnel at the Place de L'Alma. By now bodyguard Rees-Jones had buckled into his seat belt, but he was the only one.

Diana and Dodi aboard the Jonikal, August 1997

Diana and Dodi plagued by the press on holiday

Diana pleads with paparazzi

Hounded by the press

Mohammed al Fayed and Dodi Fayed

Brooke Shields and Dodi

Mercedes is removed from crash scene

Sunday Mirror August, 1997

Entrance to Pont de L'Alma tunnel

Computer simulation of Mercedes brushing white car

Mercedes veers out of control

Mercedes hits pillar number thirteen

Car finally comes to rest

Scene of the crash

Diana's coffin leaves Paris hospital

Estimates vary of the speed of the car at this point. The speed was certainly very fast, but early figures of over 120 mph (193kph) were wrong. The skid marks on the roadway in the Pont de L'Alma tunnel tell part of the story of what finally happened.

Paul's car and its precious occupants at first swerved violently to the right before control was regained—the skid marks stop. Then the car went into a second skid for thirty-two meters, hitting the thirteenth pillar—an impact which virtually destroyed the front of the car and threw it across the road.

It ended facing the wrong way against the wall of the tunnel. Dodi and Henri Paul were killed instantly, Diana was alive but semiconscious, and Rees-Jones was alive, conscious, and grievously wounded, with half his face literally hanging off.

As Henri Paul slumped forward, his body pressed against the steering wheel, and while the echoes of the crash quieted, the howling of the horn could be heard emerging eerily from the smoke and steam of the wrecked vehicle.

Chapter Six

Pictures of Greed

The indignities of the strip search were nothing compared to the horrors of the internal body inspection. On their hands and knees, stark naked, and with their most private regions poked and exposed by insistent policemen looking for concealed films, the paparazzi arrested at the site of the crash in the Pont de L'Alma underpass were frightened. They were barely aware that they were being held responsible for the deaths of three people, the serious injury of a fourth, and were about to become the most vilified group on earth.

For the photographers hauled in, the experience was shocking enough. For the loosely connected worldwide group of picture hunters known as the paparazzi, it was to a prove an incident of huge significance. The death of the woman who had become their golden goose would eventually prove, after the terrible screeching of torn metal and smashing glass of the crash had died down, to have sounded the death knell of the whole paparazzi profession itself.

There are still celebrity snappers outside the homes of the wealthy and on the pavements outside the clubs of the glitteratti, but the fabulous money earned by some during their 'Princess days' are over and the conditions under which they are allowed to operate have been circumscribed by changes in the laws of many countries.

Already in the early hours of Sunday morning, August 31, 1997, the world's media was pounding out stories of a Princess and her glamorous, wealthy, playboy lover, hounded to death by the paparazzi. The evidence appeared to be indisputable. It was obvious, or appeared to be obvious, that the freelance photographers who had increasingly made the Princess' life a misery for a decade or more had finally chased her to her death.

Indeed, it would seem to millions around the globe that it was not just the paparazzi who were responsible, but the media as a whole, who had built up Diana and paid exorbitant sums for the fuzziest of pictures in the frantic race for circulation and profit, who were ultimately to blame.

This was clearly the opinion of Earl Spencer, the brother of Diana, Princess of Wales. Speaking from his South African home, he issued a statement which reflected all the bitterness both he and the rest of her blood family felt towards not only the photographers, but to all the world's press:

'I would say that I always believed the press would kill her in the end. But not even I could imagine that they would take such a direct hand in her death as seems to be the case. It would appear that . . . every publication that has paid for intrusive and exploitative photographs of her, encouraging greedy and ruthless individuals to risk everything in pursuit of Diana's image, has blood on their hands today.'

But the six photographers and one motorcyclist taken into custody in the early hours of Sunday, August 31, were aware of none of this. They had been rounded up in the underpass itself. Now they were all in the cells of the Palais de Justice, on the Ile de la Cité, a large island in the middle of the River Seine. It is world famous for the magnificent cathedral of Nôtre Dame but better known to Parisians for the massive buildings of the central law court of the City and the home to the Judiciary Police.

Earlier they had been taken from the crash site, first to a police station in the boulevard de Courcelles, where they were formally charged, and then to the Hôpital Val de Grace for compulsory blood tests.

Later in the week following the crash, a further three photographers who had left the scene before the arrival of the police walked into a police station following massive publicity and calls to give themselves up and were formally questioned and charged.

Initially there were two charges leveled against the paparazzi: involuntary homicide and failure to help at the scene. It was said they had driven in a manner which had actually caused the crash and subsequently they had failed to render any assistance to the dead and dying in the Mercedes.

The charge of involuntary homicide in France is equivalent to a manslaughter charge in Britain and is spelled out in the country's penal code as 'causing by clumsiness, imprudence, lack of attention, negligence or by failure to observe legal safety requirements the death of another.' The second charge is covered by the 'Good Samaritan' clause in the penal code which is described as a deliberate failure to aid a person in danger, or a deliberate failure to summon assistance.

The men under arrest on that first night were Laszlo Veres, a fifty-year-old independent photographer; Romauld Rat, at twenty-four the youngest of the group and working for the Gamma agency; and his motorcycle driver, thirty-two-year-old Stephane Darmon, also with Gamma. Then there was Serge Arnal, thirty-five, with Stills; Christian Martinez, forty-one, with the Angeli agency; Nikola Arsov, thirty-eight, with the Sipa agency; and Jacques Langevin, at forty-four the eldest of the agency photographers, with Sygma.

Early reports of the role of the photographers were contradictory. A number of witnesses interviewed by the police immediately after the crash reported a large motorcycle following closely behind the Mercedes, and at least one of them reported a motorcycle with two passengers.

This would appear to be a reference to Romauld Rat with his agency driver, who were later to admit to being first on the scene, although this may not necessarily be the case. For yet another witness reported a motorcycle following the Mercedes which slowed down, passed the crashed vehicle, and then accelerated away. Little further has been heard about this motorbike during the course of the subsequent investigations, and could yet prove significant to the events leading up to the crash.

Several witnesses interviewed within hours of the event claimed that the paparazzi were right behind the car or even in front of it. This was vigorously denied by the photographers following the Mercedes in motor cars or scooters, who quickly claimed that they were neither surrounding the car nor involved in the crash.

The crucial question which arises is whether there was just one large motorcycle or two. The evidence is either contradictory or unsatisfactory. Romauld Rat is known to have stopped at the crash site but was certainly not the Mercedes' tail. If there was another then it disappeared immediately from the scene and has never been traced.

In the seconds following the crash, there was a confused and appalling scene. Even if most of the paparazzi had been a hundred yards or more behind the Mercedes they would have arrived within seconds.

There followed a feeding frenzy of picture-taking and even fighting by the photographers, which horrified other witnesses who were there soon after. First there was Romauld Rat and his driver Stephane Darmon, who parked their Honda 650 machine beyond the crash, running back to see what had happened.

Rat was not helped by the unfortunate Anglo-Saxon meaning of his name, and he was to get worldwide publicity for his actions, especially when witnesses identified him as behaving in a particularly wild manner at the scene. He was also named as the photographer involved in a scuffle with bodyguards earlier in the day outside Dodi Fayed's Paris apartment.

He freely admitted opening the rear door of the Mercedes and claimed he attempted to take the pulse of the Princess. It was this single action which more than anything turned public opinion against the paparazzi. A friend of Dodi and the Princess later said that the very thought of this man reaching into the wrecked car and putting his hand on her neck to take her pulse 'makes your flesh creep.'

The same unnamed friend was also quoted as saying that this was a man who had physically frightened the Princess and who she worried about. Rat has since claimed that his only thought at the time was compassion for the victims of the crash, how he could help, and that he only started to take pictures after the first emergency services arrived. It is also a point of some interest that Rat was the only one there at the time who had any first-aid training.

Next on the scene was Christian Martinez, one of the few happy to call himself 'paparazzi' and a self-confessed hardman. Although below average height, Martinez has spent years in the gym pumping iron and building muscles. Admired by some for his 'give no quarter' approach to the business, he had an uncompromising attitude that had never endeared him to colleagues, who disliked and maybe feared his readiness to push every incident to the limits, even to resort to violence to get his picture. 'Truculent' and 'mean spirited' were just two descriptions of him by a French reporter.

Rat and Martinez were allegedly involved in some of the ugliest scenes in the tunnel at the Pont de L'Alma that night. Early witness reports of fights between the paparazzi identified these two as the main culprits. In fact, there were further allegations of even worse behavior.

There were complaints that when the first police arrived the photographers actively blocked them. A report from one officer claimed that they were 'virulent, objectionable, and pushy, continuing to take photos and wilfully obstructing the officer from assisting the victim.'

One, later identified as Martinez, allegedly shouted out a complaint about being interrupted. In one version this appeared as: 'You really piss me off, let me do my work. At least in Sarajevo the cops let us work.' This later proved a rather odd statement for there was no evidence that he had worked in the war zone.

Based on these reports and others from the police and independent witnesses, there was a recommendation from the chief Paris prosecutor, Gabriel Bestard, that of the seven men taken into custody that night, Rat and Martinez should be kept in prison. Investigating Judge Hervé Stephan decided against this advice, but imposed a bail fee of £12,000 ($19,800), took away their press cards and driving licenses, and instructed them not to leave the country.

If at that stage in the police investigations it appeared that the paparazzi were leading players in the cause of the crash, the evidence started to crumble once news of the blood alcohol count of driver Henri Paul filtered into world consciousness. But what about the other claim that the paparazzi had failed to give assistance to the dead and dying?

Although not a felony in France, it is a criminal charge and can be punishable by up to five years in jail and a fine of up to ₤60,000 ($100,000). The evidence for this charge is that not one of the group first on the scene called an emergency telephone line for police or ambulances.

It later emerged that Serge Arnal, the Stills agency photographer, had tried to call an emergency number on his mobile phone but failed to get through. It seems at that point he did not try again, perhaps worrying that he would be too late to take his own pictures.

All the others claimed to believe that someone else had telephoned and that they were under the impression that emergency services were on their way. It is a claim which is virtually impossible to establish one way or another, but the reports suggest that the frenzy of activity could have put all thoughts of anything but getting their pictures completely out of their minds, and the possibility of formal charges being made remains open.

The fact that few pictures have appeared in the world's press is testimony to the prompt action of the French police on the night of the crash. Above all else, the strip searches and the humiliating internal body examinations were aimed at discovering and confiscating any film taken that night. The pictures processed by the police became an essential tool in the investigation process and were successful in establishing much of the truth of the paparazzi statements.

When one photographer, for example, claimed to have been late on the scene, he was confronted with pictures showing the car but none of his competitors, and was forced to confess that perhaps he had been one of the first to arrive. Accusations that Rat had been 'groveling' around in the car taking his pictures were confounded when his prints showed no shots inside the vehicle at all. Few suspects carry such clear evidence of their activities.

Not all the pictures were captured that night by the authorities. A number of photographers left the scene before the police gained control of the situation, and a desperate hunt began to find out who they were and what had happened to their pictures.

Intense questioning over two days at the Palais de Justice on the Ile de la Cité had established just who had been among the group of paparazzi. One of those who turned themselves in late was Serge Benhamou, known by celebrity chauffeurs as a difficult man to shake off even though he cruises Paris on a Honda Lada scooter. He is generally regarded as more of a celebrity snapper, albeit a very well-informed one, than a dyed-in-the-wool paparazzi. Among the first to arrive on the scene, he also left early because he found the crash emotionally difficult to handle, and he called his colleague Laszlo Veres on a mobile phone to take his place in the tunnel.

Some believed his rapid departure was an attempt to be the earliest in the world marketplace with his pictures, but he was later to be quoted as saying that once he knew that people were dead he did not want to see his pictures, because 'It is a horrible memory.'

Veres arrived some minutes after Benhamou had left and was among those caught up in the police trawl. Benhamou is thought to be the anonymous photographer interviewed on the German Television Network Pro-7 three days after the crash in which a defense of the paparazzi's actions was put forward on the grounds that ' ... we are not guilty because that is part of the game of life. The paparazzo is someone who offers pictures to the world for millions of people who wouldn't have any access. There are millions of people who buy these newspapers to have a small glimpse into the lives of these people. That is our profession.'

The other two photographers who went to the police on September 5 were David Oderkerken and Fabrice Chassery. Both work for Laurent Sola, head of LS Presse, generally recognized as a genuine paparazzi agency. Both are well known on the celebrity-snapper scene in Paris and arrived in the tunnel under the Pont de L'Alma in separate cars hard on the heels of Rat, Martinez, and Arnal.

Some would say their approach was more professional than that of the hapless Rat, for while he was taking the pulse of the Princess, they quickly shot off several rolls of film before leaping back in their cars and slipping away moments before the arrival of the police.

The pictures these two took of the emergency services arriving at the scene and especially those of the paramedics working on the Princess herself started a storm of activity in the agency office. The films were quickly processed by Sola and the best were scanned into his computers and transmitted directly to the agency's London office.

As news of the pictures spread across the world's media networks, offers poured in from all points of the globe. Within hours, Sola had recorded offers of more than a million pounds from eager buyers in Britain, Spain, Italy, and Germany. One American magazine alone is reputed to have offered $250,000 (£150,000) that night for rights to the pictures.

It was yet another full-fledged feeding frenzy. The situation was to change again quite dramatically a few hours later just as the first stories of the crash and Dodi's death were appearing on agency wires. Realizing that there were treacherous waters ahead, the two photographers contacted Sola to suggest that instead of being sold, perhaps the pictures should be destroyed.

Sola quickly recognized the strength of their argument, wiped his computer images, and handed in the negatives to the police. By this time the police were touring other agencies warning them that to own photos or cause pictures of the crash scene to be published could be a felony obstructing the investigation with penalties of both jail terms and large fines. At the same time they were warned not to destroy any negatives.

In London, it would appear that a different approach was adopted by the authorities. During the night of September 3, intruders broke into the flat of Sipa photographer and agent Lionel Cherruault in North West London. They were professionals who knew exactly what they were looking for. Ignoring valuables, televisions, videos—all the usual targets of casual burglars—they were interested only in his computer.

Working in the room next to where Cherruault and his wife were sleeping, they 'confiscated' two external computer hard disk drives together with a laptop computer. The only other items stolen were credit cards and some cash, and the keys to a Mitsubishi Spacewagon in which the burglars made their escape.

It was what happened next which gives the story a sinister overtone. For after calling the police over during the night, Cherruault was astonished to be told the next morning by detectives that he 'had not been burgled.' Twenty-four hours later, the Mitsubishi was found near the Stonebridge Park council estate in North West London.

Police investigations revealed nothing—no fingerprints and nothing to point to the nighttime intruders. For the police to suggest that this was not a burglary is a misuse of language. The photographer certainly had his flat and his property abused, and the valuable computer equipment was never discovered. By any description that is burglary. But it was made crystal clear that no action would, or could, be taken by the police.

It would seem that Mr. Cherruault has every reason to conclude that his night visitors were members of an official clandestine organization trying to intercept pictures of the crash. However, strangely enough, the Sipa photographer in the tunnel that night, Nikola Arsov, failed to switch on his electronic flash and produced not a single picture that was publishable.

Despite the best efforts of the police and other authorities in both France and Britain, some of the pictures taken that night did escape censorship. One fuzzy picture very quickly appeared on the Internet, although after it was published on the front page of the French daily *France Soir* it proved to be a fake. Other pictures were published in Germany and Italy, but it would seem that for once public opinion was not prepared to stomach such gory images and a rare display of taste and scruples prevented most other papers from publishing pictures.

Chapter Seven

Flying High

Skimming above the green fields of Brittany, young Henri Paul could allow his thoughts to wander. Although he had only recently taken up flying at the age of sixteen, it had already captured his imagination. His instructor was confident in his skill, he appeared to have a real feel for the tiny aircraft, and he reveled in the pure joy of the freedom of flying. 'This will be my future,' he thought, allowing the imagination of youth to run through the options. Would he fly jet fighters for the military, maybe, or should he train for a commercial pilot's license? Whichever way it went, he was happy to know it was a fine way to escape a humdrum life and could easily lead to a well-rewarded career.

Henri Paul also loved the freedom of sailing, another sport he embraced enthusiastically from his hometown of Lorient on the southern tip of the Breton peninsula. As well as being a busy fishing harbor, the safe estuary waters of Lorient have long made it a favorite base for the yachtsmen who pack the town every weekend. Although sailing did not capture the imagination of young Henri in the same way that flying had, he was just as adept in the handling skills of a lively dinghy, slicing through the waves on a breezy day, yelling aloud his delight at the exhilaration of the sport.

For Paul, the dreams of youth were never to find expression in his career. Although he continued to enjoy the delights of flying and sailing for the rest of his life, poor eyesight was finally to prove an insurmountable obstacle to his hopes of converting a sport into a worthwhile living. If it were not for this misfortune of fate, Paul may never have become a key player in one of the greatest tragedies of the twentieth century as the man who became reviled as an allegedly debauched, drunken driver responsible for the death of the world's adored Princess.

His crimes were even worse in the eyes of those who believed that the real guilt lay with the media intrusions into her life, and especially that worldwide band of desperadoes, the paparazzi. The extraordinary level of alcohol in Paul's body was a gift of incalculable value to the whole happy band of 'sad-snappers,' diverting the weight of the investigations into an entirely different direction.

As events unfolded during the late summer of 1997, that direction became increasingly focused on the life of Paul. And what quickly became clear to everyone involved—the official investigators, the private investigators hired by the Al Fayed family, and the many investigative reporters dispatched by the world's press and other news media—was that every discovery about Henri's private life served simply to expose another mystery. For the simple lad from Lorient had become a complex personality. His friends were compartmentalized into what could look suspiciously similar to a cell structure, and the excessive neatness of his private life extended into his business world to keep 'Chinese walls' between his diverse official duties.

Many questions were thrown up around the life of Paul. Was he a chronic alcoholic? Was he being treated for depression?

Did he take drugs? Why were vast sums of money deposited in his bank account shortly before the crash? Did he deal in drugs? Did he trade information with the police? Was he in the pay of another, unknown, organization? If so, what was he paid for? Was he selling the secrets of the rich and famous? What role did the 'mystery' blond play in his life ? Was he bisexual, with an interest in the murky world of Paris homosexuals and transsexuals?

Somewhere within this maze of mysteries could lie the truth behind the death of Diana, Princess of Wales.

There was little in Paul's life to suggest he would become a key figure in such bizarre world-shattering events until the time he joined the security team at the Paris Ritz. One of five boys, he was born on July 3, 1956 into a respectable working-class Lorient family. His father was a municipal worker, and his mother a housewife and part-time teacher with a deep love of music. They always remained deeply proud of him, and were convinced that not only was he not an alcoholic, but that he could not have been driving under the influence of alcohol.

At the Lycée St. Louis he is remembered as a respectful, studious boy who coped easily with his classes. He passed the demanding tests for his Baccalaureat in mathematics and science and showed a talent for languages, learning English and some German. At the same time he trained as a classical pianist at the music conservatory and eventually gained his prized flying license at the age of nineteen before going on to achieve the demanding qualification to fly by instruments.

For some time he was able to turn his love of flying into more than just a hobby, earning money as a flying instructor. In 1979 he left for the French Airforce base at Rochefort for a compulsory one year tour of duty in the armed forces, where to his disappointment he was assigned to security duties, an

echo of his final, fateful job. What he wanted, of course, was
to be accepted for pilot officer training, which might eventually lead to the excitement of a jet fighter squadron. It would
seem that only his eyesight let him down.

He was to remain an Air Force Reserve Officer until 1992,
but after his conscription Paul moved to Paris, deciding like
many of his contemporaries at the Lycée St. Louis that the
provincial life of Lorient had little to offer an ambitious youth.
He quickly found employment with Emeraude Marine, a yacht
agency and ships' chandlers specializing in catamarans, close
to the center of Paris. Here his knowledge of sailing from his
youthful days in Lorient must have been a real bonus.

The work clearly suited him for he was to stay with the
company for six years, and he was later to buy a catamaran
with a group of friends. During this period and maybe reflecting his airforce experience, he was recommended as a security consultant to the Ritz Hotel and worked part-time with the
architect who was overseeing refurbishment and upgrading
work.

There was a measured orderliness to his life in Paris at this
time. He was a man with many acquaintances and was part of
a small, tightly knit group of friends, many of them Bretons
like Henri himself. Every Wednesday four of them would gather
at the Grand Colbert restaurant on the rue Vivienne, where
they regularly occupied the same table. Henri was considerate
to the staff and was known as a light drinker and lover of fine
food, particularly seafood.

He was a man who liked routine: Saturday nights would usually find him out for dinner at the home of a family friend and
Saturday mornings were jealously guarded for tennis. At other
times the four friends would go bowling or sailing. In many
ways it was an active life for a city dweller, and it was clear

from his stocky, muscular build that Paul was a man who kept himself fit and strong.

In fact he was somewhat paranoid about his health, and often fussed over imagined illnesses, consulting friends for remedies for which they believed he had no real use. Sometimes he irritated them in other ways, particularly when buying hi-fi and audio-visual equipment for his immaculate flat. It was never simple for Paul. Everything had to be assessed and examined, the specialist magazines consulted and fine comparisons made between the competing equipment which had caught his eye. It could take him months to reach a decision, wearying his friends in the process.

Although Henri never married, and never presented his mother with grandchildren, he was a man who needed feminine company. And it wasn't difficult to find. Many girls were to drift through his life, for he was an attractive and active man with a knowledge of fine wine and foods, an entertaining wit, and an inquiring mind.

Few relationships lasted long, perhaps due to his compulsion to compartmentalize his life, or maybe it was a reflection of his possessiveness. His male friends knew little about his girlfriends, his girlfriends knew little about his work, his colleagues only understood that part of his activities which concerned them, and rarely, if ever, did he discuss his private life with them.

Apart from his mother, the most important women to Henri were Laurence Pujol and her daughter Samentha, who shared his flat—and his life—for four years. He met Laurence when she worked in the personnel office at the Ritz, and they were quickly attracted to each other. It took only a month or two before Pujol and her daughter moved into Paul's flat, in a fashionable area of Paris close to the Arc de Triomphe.

The arrival of a lively child in the middle of the infamous 'terrible two' years was a cultural shock for the long-time bachelor, but Paul quickly grew to love the child as much as the mother, and was proud to play an active role in her upbringing. As she grew from babyhood to budding schoolchild he would enjoy helping her learn to read, teaching her to play computer games and the piano, and taking her out on weekends, maybe flying from the airstrip outside Paris.

It was a happy domestic scene, perhaps one of the happiest periods of Henri's life. But sadly it was not to last. For Laurence, perhaps it was not what she wanted in a long-term relationship. It would seem that the sharp city-girl found the attentions of her lover too restrictive.

Whatever the background to the rift in their partnership, it all came to a head in 1992 when Laurence and Samentha left the flat. It was not to be a complete break, for the two kept in touch; occasionally they enjoyed romantic nights out, and Henri would still take Samentha on trips. But it was a drifting relationship, clearly not what he needed, and it was to lead to a dark spell for Paul.

During 1997, there were reports of a new lady in Paul's life, young (in her mid-twenties), blond, and from his home country of Brittany. They would meet mostly on a Sunday for lunch and clearly enjoyed each other's company. She was, sadly, waiting for him at their regular restaurant on the Sunday after the crash, clearly knowing nothing about the terrible events of the previous night. But it was a discreet relationship. Monsieur Paul did not introduce her to his group of close friends, and neither was she taken home to meet his parents and family. The relationship remains a mystery.

There was yet another lady in his life whose very existence appears to have come as a shock to both friends and family. It is reported that when Paul's parents were carrying out the sad task of winding up his Paris affairs a quiet lady knocked at the door and handed in a key to the apartment, saying that she would not be needing it again. She did not give her name.

If there was stress in his life at this stage it wasn't immediately obvious to his friends or colleagues. He continued to enjoy the easy lifestyle of the City bon-vivant, continued to fly himself and other Breton friends to Lorient on trips home, and tackled his work with all his usual enthusiasm. But it is also around this time that he may have started taking prescription drugs to treat depression, although it never seemed he needed them.

Many friends recall him being prone to bouts of depression at various stages in his life, but never sufficiently severe to require drug treatment, and it has been reported that Laurence Pujol never saw any signs of drugs around the flat during the time she lived there.

It is also possible that he started to drink more than had been his custom. Although he enjoyed a reputation as something of a connoisseur of fine wines, there were few suggestions at this stage in his life that he was a drunk. After the crash, investigators discovered only one incriminating piece of evidence pointing to secret drinking. An anonymous note from a disenchanted employee was discovered in a drawer of his desk at the hotel claiming that all the staff committee, of which Paul was a member, were a 'bunch of good-for-nothing crooks and the Breton (presumably Paul) is the worst of all.' It continued, as described by the police: 'an individual nicknamed the Breton rakes in millions and drinks alcohol all day long.'

The move from shop assistant in a ship's chandlers to security consultant at one of the world's leading hotels does seem an all too fortuitous leap for the young Paul, even allowing for his somewhat limited experience of a year in 'security' in the French air force. It is a move which has not been satisfactorily explained. The initial link came through his friendship with detective Jacques Pocher, a member of the Judicial Police in Paris who was the go-between with Claude Roulet, assistant manager and the executive at the Ritz responsible for establishing a security department at the hotel.

Initially acting as a consultant to the architect refurbishing the hotel, Paul must have done outstanding work, for when in 1986 the hotel's security department was finally established he was appointed assistant director. And when, in the following year, his boss Jean Hocquet resigned, Paul became acting head responsible for a staff of around twenty people.

By any standards this is impressive progress, especially in a field in which he had no formal training and only apparently the briefest experience. It suggests that he had a natural talent both for security and personnel management, that his face fitted in the hierarchy of the hotel in a remarkable way, or that he had friends or connections with a vested interest in his career. Just what that vested interest may have been and who the friends or contacts were and where they connected to the Ritz Hotel are questions which certainly deserve further explanation.

One indication may be Paul's many banks accounts and the large sums of money deposited in them. It is estimated he earned £20,000 ($33,000) annually from the Ritz but apart from small deposits in accounts in his hometown, he patronized three banks in Paris—Barclays, Banque Nationale, and Banque D'Epargne—and had eleven accounts. Five payments of £4,000 ($6,500) were made into one of them shortly before he died, and in total he had savings of a surprising £122,000 ($200,000).

His close friend Paul Garrec believes the money came from the French and foreign security services for whom he was an important freelance agent. Garrec said his position at the Ritz made a valuable contact, but he did not know if Paul was an 'asset' before he joined the Ritz and got his job on that score.

It is an anomaly that after Paul's early surge to seniority in the Ritz security section he was later twice overlooked for the final important promotion to Head of Security: first when Joseph Geoddet was replaced by Jean Hocquet and then when Hocquet himself resigned.

If Paul was not universally popular with his subordinates in the hotel, as suggested by the anonymous note discovered by the investigating magistrates' team, he appeared to enjoy the complete confidence of the hotel bosses and, according to reports, he displayed an almost exaggerated respect for hierarchy. His immediate superiors at the hotel at the time of the crash were Frank Klein, the president of the hotel and chief executive of the Al Fayed interests in Paris, including the 'Royal' property previously occupied by the late Duke and Duchess of Windsor in the Bois du Boulogne; Claude Rolet, who had given the young Paul his first opening at the Ritz; and Franco Mora, the hotel manager. Paul was admired by all three for his very positive approach to any task assigned to him, for his absolute loyalty, and also for his willingness never to question any work assignment.

Also very much in his favor was the fact that Paul had established a close relationship with the Fayeds. He enjoyed the confidence of both father and son and it is a matter of some conjecture whether Dodi had personally requested that Paul drive himself and Princess Diana on the night of the crash. Certainly Paul was at the bottom of the steps when the couple stepped off their private jet in Paris and was warmly greeted by both the Princess and Dodi. He then drove the Land Rover which formed part of the convoy escorting the party to Dodi's apartments in the center of Paris.

The response from the Al Fayeds in London and the executives of the Paris Ritz to criticism of Paul was one of outrage. When the first suggestions filtered through that he was under the influence of alcohol on the night of the crash, the expressions of disbelief are proof enough of that.

As already stated, his parents were totally unaware of any suggestion he was a long-term serious drinker, although this in itself may not prove very much, for he had been living away from home for many years. The medical he took for his pilot's license just two days before the crash is a different matter. It exposed no alcohol-related problems even though the tests included both blood and urine samples.

Equally importantly, his long-term live-in girlfriend Laurence Pujol did not regard him as a heavy drinker, was also surprised that he was taking any form of antidepressant drugs, and claimed that she had never seen prescription drugs around the apartment. Then there is the testimony of his coterie of close friends, and from the regular circuit of bars he would frequent in the area of his flat and his work.

At least two of these friends, Garrec and Dominique Mélo, members of the regular group who got together for dinner each Saturday, remember Paul as a man who enjoyed an aperitif, a glass of good quality wine, and the occasional glass of Ricard following a meal. What they do not remember is a man who would drink to excess and certainly not one who ever lost control of his faculties because of drinking.

Although driving was not part of Paul's regular duties at the hotel and did not feature in his job description, he had been sent to courses at the Mercedes driving school and occasionally was the selected driver for the Al Fayeds when they were in town. His colleagues and friends remember him as a cautious driver and none can ever recall him driving recklessly or showing the influence of drinking.

It is interesting also that no evidence, apart from the body-alcohol level measured after the crash, exists that he was drinking heavily on the vital Saturday. Hotel records reveal that it was past 7 P.M. before he went off duty, having finally escorted Dodi and Princess back from the airport, and he was back in the hotel by 10:30 that night. A heavy drinker could certainly get drunk in that time, and it would be likely to show, but there is no evidence that Paul went out on a bender.

He possibly had a drink in one or two bars but no one in those he frequented has reported seeing him drinking before his return to the Ritz. When he left the hotel in the early evening it seems he went off in his black Mini to his flat in rue des Petits Champs, just a few minutes away. He was seen to park in rue Chabanais round the corner, outside the lesbian bar Champmesle. The barman at Le Bourgogne, another pub near the entrance to his block of flats, remembers seeing him as he passed by and having a chat, but Paul had nothing to drink before shaking hands and departing.

It is evident that he went home in this period because he changed his jacket: photographs and video footage prove this. The next apparent sighting was just before he returned to the Ritz, after 10 P.M. when the female owner of the Champmesle saw him pick up his Mini and he waved to her. Again, he did not have a drink but drove off.

It is possible that he had one or two drinks at several bars during the 'missing' three and a half-hours, but he was a familiar figure in the vicinity of the hotel and of his apartment, and it seems likely that somebody would have spotted him. No one has come forward, so the only evidence of alcohol consumption is two glasses of Ricard, the aniseed-based drink, which he consumed in the Ritz bar after he returned.

The other possibility is that he was drinking on his own at home, something which has not been proven one way or another, although some partly filled bottles were found there. Reports from members of the staff at the hotel and from one or two paparazzi that he looked drunk on the night in question remain unconfirmed. Some said he had trouble parking his Mini when he arrived for the extra late-night stint of duty.

But his immediate colleagues flatly deny any evidence of drunkenness. Bodyguard Trevor Rees-Jones, trained to spot unusual behavior, has stated quite unequivocally that he appeared absolutely normal that night. He must also have appeared normal to Dodi Fayed when he specifically chose Paul to be his driver.

Equally puzzling is the Ritz video footage of Paul in the Ritz just before he set off on his last journey with his passengers. He shows no sign of inebriation, just as Rees-Jones said. At one point he steps deftly down a flight of stairs, turns on his heels, and starts chatting with a Ritz staff member. He looks erect and respectful when speaking to Dodi and Diana. He was most certainly not rolling drunk as much media coverage has deduced from the blood tests.

After a number of delays, Paul was eventually buried in Lorient on September 20, three weeks after the crash. To his family and friends in the seaside town he will never be remembered as the guilty drunk who killed a princess and her wealthy lover. What his epitaph will be to the rest of the world is still undecided. It may yet be proven that he was more sinned against than sinning. It all hinges on whether the blood tests can be relied upon.

Chapter Eight

Foul Play?

Premeditated treachery and coup plots happen in third-world countries but surely never in Britain, one of the oldest democracies. Mutterings and talk there might be, but could it go any further? Could orders have filtered down from on high to have a Princess and her boyfriend eliminated?

All over the globe, this is the language of the crank and that much-derided phenomenon, the conspiracy theorist. But, as the authors have discovered, in the instance of Diana's death, the belief in a sinister plot runs much wider.

A persistent story has been lurking within the British SAS, the renowned Special Air Service units, that the crash that killed Henri Paul and his passengers was pinned on them. One soldier said, 'That is what we keep hearing. It was a typical SAS-type operation and some of us are very unhappy about it.'

He was not suggesting that orders had come down from above to stage an accident in the Paris tunnel, but, he said, it was possible that the sentiments of, say, certain members of the Royal family and their irritation with Diana's recent behavior had been misconstrued, with disastrous consequences.

Perhaps inevitably the other persistent rumor is that MI5 or MI6 had a hand in the accident. It would not be the first time that a group from within Britain's security services had exceeded their brief and taken action, erroneously thinking it would ease pressure on the Monarchy if a disaster befell a vexing subject. History records that similar careless talk sealed the fate of Archbishop Thomas à Becket, murdered by four soldiers after Henry VIII famously muttered, 'Will no one rid me of this turbulent priest?'

This chapter pauses in the discussion of the events directly concerned with Diana and Dodi's death to examine evidence that the Princess may not have been speaking wildly when she voiced fears that she might one day be a target of her 'enemy' the British Establishment. It may seem inconceivable, but one does not have to delve too far into the past to discover direct evidence of coup plots and groups operating outside the law to protect what they perceive as 'good and true.' If Dodi and Di were targeted, it is in these people's direction the finger of suspicion should first be pointed, although, no doubt, they are clever enough to have covered their tracks.

In modern times, a name that often comes up when there is talk of plots and counter-plots is that of Colonel David Stirling, founder of the SAS during World War Two and a figure held in great suspicion by the left. In a rare interview before he died, Stirling told the authors about a meeting and dinner he attended at a royal palace in late 1974 or early 1975, hosted by a senior member of the monarchy. Prince Charles' uncle, Lord Louis Mountbatten, attended. There were ten others representing the security services, including the heads of MI6 and MI5.

Stirling said everyone was present in an 'unofficial' capacity, but pointed out that all military officers swear an oath of allegiance to the Crown: 'They regard the Queen as the ultimate authority.' He implied that the feelings of Royals held greater sway in the thoughts of those present than that of the elected government, and said that the meeting was convened to discuss the grave state of the country, which at the time was riven by strikes and only just recovering from a three-day week in industry because of power shortages.

Why was Stirling invited to this gathering? He had retired long ago from military service. However, he was at the time running a private company employed by various secret services to carry out 'deniable' operations in various world 'trouble spots,' and his links with the military and particularly with the SAS were excellent. More significantly, Stirling had appointed himself leader of GB75, a secretive private task force which was ready to take over utilities in times of industrial crisis.

The talk at this powerful grouping of Establishment figures was of the need for intervention in political developments, and the question of how to do this by force was on the agenda. Stirling said he addressed the meeting on his previous relevant experience in dealing with such matters and told how he had once mounted an operation in Tripoli designed to spark-off a coup d'état. He also described another similar operation he had masterminded somewhere else, but was not specific about the location.

It was clear from Stirling that the group was discussing the possibility of unseating Harold Wilson and replacing him with a more acceptable leader. Such talk was not new. A year earlier, a figure none other than the head of the civil service, Sir William Armstrong, attended a Ditchley Foundation conference of rising politicos and administrators and talked of the need for intervention to stop the mayhem of industrial unrest and Labour coming to power. The passion with which Armstrong spoke led some of those present to believe he was advocating a coup. He was diagnosed as being 'under strain' and went to Lord Rothschild's villa in the Caribbean to recuperate.

Readers will recall that the retired Assistant Director of MI5,

Peter Wright, author of *Spycatcher,* blew the whistle on political meddling by his own colleagues. His ghosted autobiography exposes many MI5 activities which were highly dubious: 'For five years we bugged and burgled our way across London at the State's behest, while pompous bowler-hatted civil servants in Whitehall pretended to look the other way.'

He recounts how the CIA raised with him the delicate subject of 'wet affairs,' the name for assassinations. One senior US agent said: 'We're developing a new capability in the Company to handle these kinds of problems, and we're in the market for the requisite expertise.' Apparently, the prime target was Third World leaders. Wright replied: 'The French! Have you tried them? It's more their type of thing, you know.... We're out of that game. We're the junior partner in the alliance, remember? It's your responsibility now.'

Wright tells of how he was in his office in 1974, when several officers entered looking very concerned. 'Wilson's a bloody menace,' said one of them. Wright recalled: 'It was not the first time I had heard that particular sentiment. Feelings had run high in MI5 during 1968. There had been an effort to stir up trouble for Wilson then, largely because the *Daily Mirror* tycoon Cecil King, who was a long-time agent of ours, made it clear he would publish anything MI5 might care to leak in his direction. It was all part of Cecil King's 'coup' which he was convinced would bring down the Labour Government and replace it with a coalition led by Lord Mountbatten.'

Wright said that events in 1974 grew yet more serious: 'The plan was simple. In the run-up to the general election which, given the level of instability in Parliament, must be due in a matter of months, MI5 would arrange for selective details of the intelligence about leading Labour Party figures, but especially Wilson, to be leaked to sympathetic pressmen. Using our contacts in the Press and among union officials word of the material contained in MI5 files and the fact that Wilson was considered a security risk would be passed around.'

The 'spycatcher' refused to participate but the plan went into action. An investigation by two BBC journalists, Barrie Penrose and Roger Courtiour, related in the book, The Pencourt File, showed that an extensive propaganda smear campaign run by Wright's colleagues had careered out of control. False information about Labour politicians was spread, including to news agencies in the United States. MI5 rewrote and then issued fake speeches purporting to have been drafted by Labour MPs, and bank statements were doctored to suggest MPs were taking handouts and backhanders.

It emerged that the campaign was modeled on a CIA-inspired operation known as Psy-Ops (Psychological Operations), employed in Vietnam to destabilize the communist regime. MI5 had first employed the techniques in Northern Ireland.

Wright also revealed that at the same time a freelance dirty-tricks operation was set up, possibly the same organization that Colonel David Stirling was advising. In the early 1970s, Wright had grown disenchanted with MI5, where he was being sidelined, so he was thinking of leaving the service. He said that he was introduced to a businessman and a 'ramshackle' bunch of colleagues by his friend Viktor Rothschild, the scientist and former MI5 officer.

Wright recalled: 'They were retired people from various branches of intelligence and security organizations whose best years were well behind them. There were others too, mainly businessmen who seemed thrilled to be in the same room as spies....'

The leader told Wright that they represented a group well

endowed with funds who were worried about the state of the country. 'He said they were working to prevent the return of a Labour Government to power. It could spell the end of all the freedoms we know and cherish.'

Wright said that he declined the offer of joining this shadowy group but also that the story justified Harold Wilson's subsequent concern about the possibility of a coup against him. His suspicions had been alerted when troops dramatically moved in to surround Heathrow airport and set up checkpoints in a joint operation with the police. Wilson, to his chagrin, had not been told about the exercise in advance or of any apparent terrorist threat that might justify such an action.

GB75 was not the only private 'army' being formed in this period and David Stirling was not the only army veteran making preparations. General Sir Walter Walker, former NATO Commander-in-Chief in northern Europe, sprang into prominence and became a focus of right-wing discontent. He formed a 100,000 strong civil assistance organization called Civil Assistance, led by a network of controllers many of whom were ex-military.

Civil Assistance was said to have numerous well-known supporters including Mountbatten, Airey Neave MP, and Ross McWhirter. It had originally been an offshoot of another private force, 'Unison' (no relation to the trade union), run by George Kennedy Young, a former deputy chief of MI6.

Walker issued a clarion call for a rebirth of the country and 'stronger leadership,' which we can reasonably infer was secretly supported with nods and winks by Lord Mountbatten and allied pillars of the Establishment. 'Now is the need for a rebirth of national morale under inspiring and democratically elected leadership,' Walker told a meeting in Hong Kong. 'We haven't got that leadership.' Less than democratically, he then suggested the ex-chairman of the Coal Board, Lord Robens, should lead a 'Government of national unity.'

Roy Mason, Secretary of State for Defense, attacked Walker publicly and deplored the formation of private armies. There were strong denials that these groups had sinister objectives beyond their stated aim of helping to keep the wheels of power turning in the event of a civil or industrial emergency. If that was all, it would be easy to dismiss this activity as transient mischief. However, it later emerged there was far more to all these 'preparations' than a collection of 'Colonel Blimps' playing at being soldiers again. It was reported that senior army officers at Sandhurst were openly discussing the need to actively intervene in the political process. These views were so widespread that the army was forced to write to all units warning that such talk must cease, pointing out that orders came ultimately from the Secretary of State for Defense and no other authority.

It was around this time that John Mitchell, Chairman of Cunard, was woken by an urgent phone call. He told one of the authors an extraordinary story which showed that the plotting had nearly got completely out of hand. 'In July 1975 I was at home in Henley,' Mitchell said. 'A brigadier from Camberley apologized for waking me up but said it was a matter of national importance. Would I be willing to help the authorities if my help was needed? The man mentioned they knew of my war record and felt I could be trusted. I replied I would help of course. As a patriot I could do little else. The man said I should expect a call later.'

'The call came in the middle of the night. This time it was from someone much more senior. I was told the people he was speaking on behalf of had been in touch with Sir Basil Small-peice, who was financial advisor to the Queen. He had indicated his agreement to be part of a [new] Government in the United Kingdom. I was asked if I would agree too and given a phone number to ring back on.'

Mitchell said that he rang Smallpeice the next morning to discover that he too had been woken in the middle of the night a few days earlier. After a similar initial conversation with the brigadier, he had been to a meeting in the Knightsbridge area of London. Smallpeice told Mitchell a number of high-ranking secret service agents were planning a coup and 'it was the ships they want.' In particular they wanted control of the *QE2*.

Mitchell then went to a similar meeting. 'The place looked like a house but was furnished a bit like a library. A butler brought some drinks and I was introduced to these three men in tweeds. They gave names but I cannot remember them and I don't think they were true.

'They asked me to take part in a coup. They said it would involve the army. They implied it had the highest backing. They kept asking me if the Captain of the *QE2* would obey my instructions if I ordered him to take instructions from them. I said, quite accurately, that the captain was an employee of mine and that he would do as he was told. But I said I had grave doubts about what they were doing.

'I went out of there in a state of shock. They made it quite clear they were planning an armed coup. I went to see Sir Basil Smallpeice and said what these people were doing was wrong. He agreed and suggested we tell these people no.

Mitchell recounted how he went to see Sir Michael Cary, Permanent Under-Secretary of State at the Ministry of Defense. He was later told that the matter had been dealt with. 'It was all an exercise that had got a bit out of hand.'

Mitchell said he believed the coup plan was real and not an exercise, and several years later he was still shaken by the recollection. He believes the *QE2* was earmarked as a floating prison for those members of the Government, including Harold Wilson, who would need to be 'put somewhere safe.'

Sir Basil Smallpeice would not conjecture about how the coup plan would have been effected, but he confirmed key parts of Mitchell's story, including the initial involvement of a brigadier whose name Smallpeice had written in his diary. In 1975 this officer was responsible for dealing with military prisons. He claimed that he too had been drawn into the affair with a late-night phone call. He said that he had met Sir Basil Smallpeice but he would not say what had been discussed.

Was there a link between this strange episode, the meeting where David Stirling met up with Lord Mountbatten and the security chiefs, and the group Wright was asked to join? It seems possible, and the element of bungling suggested by Mitchell and Smallpeice is equally plausible. In any event, the *QE2* never became a floating prison, the matter was carefully buried, and the Wilson Government struggled on for a while longer.

The atmosphere of political and social crisis so prevalent in 1975 gradually dispersed, as did the private armies. Or did they disperse in their entirety? There is much more recent evidence that some groups survived, secretly taking the law into their own hands.

The evidence for this comes first from within the security services itself. A man we shall call 'John,' an MI5 officer, arranged to meet Peter Hounam, one of the authors of this book. After the usual pleasantries, John produced a book. 'I want you to read this as soon as possible,' he said. 'You will find it very interesting.' Then he added: 'This is what I don't like about my job. Things sometimes go too far.'

The book was *The Feather Men,* by the explorer Sir Ranulph

Fiennes, and its fly-leaf was, to say the least, intriguing: 'Over a period of fourteen years, from 1977 until 1990, a group of hired killers known as the Clinic tracked down and killed four former British soldiers, one at a time.... Throughout those fourteen years, The Feather Men hunted the Clinic and were never far behind.... It may be that in a democracy where the taxpayers do not want an all-powerful invasive police force, there is a need for private groupings like the Feather Men. Some readers will be thankful that the Feather Men exist. Others will not.'

It was useless asking John any more questions. 'Don't be mistaken—this is not fiction, though it may seem that way,' he said. 'Just read the book and you'll see what I'm getting at.'

Ranulph Fiennes, famous for his trans-global and polar expeditions, lives on a farm on the edge of Exmoor, Devon, but he was once an army officer with the Royal Scots Greys. For much of his army career he was attached to the Special Air Service, famous for shinning down ropes and smashing through the windows of the Iranian embassy to end the terrorist siege there in May 1980. Fiennes was with 22 SAS Regiment and remained with the SAS as a territorial (part-time) officer until 1984, but it was on Monday, October 22, 1990, that he came face-to-face with 'the Clinic,' the paid assassins, in the most extraordinary circumstances.

As he did every Monday evening, Fiennes collected the black garbage bags from outside his farm house and took them a mile away by car to the council collection point. Rounding a bend, he found a black Volvo estate blocking his path. It was empty, but he spotted a light in a nearby barn and went inside to investigate, carrying a tire lever in case of trouble.

Suddenly, a voice shouted, 'Drop it!' and four torches were

shone on him. Fiennes was told to sit on a bale of straw, while one of the men set up a video camera on a tripod. A man who spoke in what appeared to be slight American accent then began to question Fiennes about the death of a rich Omani sheikh's son which had occurred when Fiennes was serving in the SAS.

Baffled as to why this menacing group were interested in an event that took place twenty-five years earlier, Fiennes nonetheless answered their questions. He had, in any case, written a book about his part in the Oman campaign and about 'Operation Snatch,' a plan to capture two communist leaders, one of whom was the Sheikh's son.

Fiennes had written about this man being killed in the operation and admitted this to his captors. The leader of the group said, 'So you admit to the murder of this man,' which Fiennes denied. He was then told to return to his car and drive slowly down a nearby hill.

Not surprisingly, Fiennes feared he was about to be killed, but suddenly there was an enormous commotion. Men with blackened faces and truncheons appeared from nowhere and proceeded to attack the mysterious group. There was a muffled scream and the sound of breaking glass, then someone tapped Fiennes on the shoulder with the reassuring comment: 'Cheer Up. They've all gone. You're in no danger.'

The following day, Fiennes learned more about the Clinic, the Feather Men, and how he had unknowingly become embroiled in a plot by the sheikh to revenge the deaths of four of his sons. All of them had been killed by British soldiers in different incidents during the Oman campaign, and the sheikh, who was a successful merchant, would be in disgrace unless he retaliated.

That much is plausible, but how the sheikh wreaked

vengeance is very difficult to accept. Allegedly acting through an agency in Earls Court, the Clinic are said to have been offered £5 million to seek out the culprits, obtain videoed confessions, and then kill them in ways that would not look like murder.

Fiennes relates how he was subsequently asked to produce a book about the Feather Men by its leader, Colonel Tommy Macpherson, an industrialist and a well-known figure in the City of London. Fiennes says the book was compiled from the stories of twenty-six people who had been involved.

One soldier is said to have been killed in a helicopter crash in Oman. Another apparently died of hypothermia while taking part in a testing march across moorland. A third died from an epileptic seizure.

But it was the fourth ex-soldier whose story is particularly pertinent to the fatal car crash that killed Diana, Princess of Wales, Dodi Fayed, and Henri Paul, and which shows, if his story is true, that no one can take the 'accident' theory for granted especially if there are suspicious factors.

Major Michael Marman, formerly with the 9th/12th Royal Lancers was driving along the A303 between London and the West Country in his Citroen 2CV in November, 1986 when a BMW travelling in the opposite direction careened across the central reservation, killing him instantly. According to Fiennes' book, Marman was the victim of an elaborate booby-trap that entailed the most meticulous planning.

Fiennes recounts how Marman had been under surveillance for several weeks. His trip along the A303 had been scheduled for some time and this, it was decided, was an ideal opportunity for staging the hit. The Clinic discovered that another car, owned by retired Air Marshall Sir Peter Horsley was due to travel in the opposite direction, and this was targeted. A member of the Clinic identified as Jake was drafted in to help, an ideal choice as it turned out, as he had spent three years training as a mechanic at Mercedes' workshops at Untertuerkheim, Germany.

Fiennes describes in detail how Horsley's BMW 728i was tampered with, and he provides a diagram of the modifications secretly made to the vehicle. He says the car was altered so that the braking system could be taken over by remote control. Radio receivers were attached to the BMW which, via other equipment, could manipulate the master break cylinder. At the crucial moment, the normal hydraulic system operating the brakes could be bypassed. Another system would take over, operating by compressed air from a tiny scuba diving cylinder ten inches long hidden in the BMW's engine compartment.

A transmitter with a joystick control used for guiding model aircraft was then tuned to activate the receivers. This was apparently installed in a dark blue Volvo estate car closely following Horsley's BMW just before the crash.

The explorer describes how on the afternoon of November 11, 1986, the trap was sprung. A Clinic member waited for Marman's 2CV, travelling at seventy mph, to converge on Horsley near Stonehenge, and then began to use the joystick control to apply the brakes of the BMW differentially. Horsley, also travelling at about seventy mph, could not control the car as it began to snake wildly. It swerved across the central reservation, striking the 2CV and causing it to concertina.

Marman died instantly, but Horsley suffered lacerations and was conscious when he was found near his car. According to Fiennes, the vehicle was later secretly stripped of any incriminating equipment, and the Clinic could congratulate itself on a successful hit. But is this bizarre story, told in minute detail by Fiennes, credible? A number of key people have backed important aspects.

One of these is the 'chief Feather Man' Colonel Tommy Macpherson, who revealed that part of the proceeds of the book went, with his blessing, to the SAS Jubilee Fund. He allowed his name to be used in the book, thereby adding credence to the existence of a *Man From UNCLE* type of organization in Britain, whose role is to combat evil groups of professional hit men.

Equally convincing is the comment of one of the Feather Men's alleged operatives, Captain David Mason, whose photograph appears in the book. He was a regular with 22 SAS Regiment before being recruited for occasional duties with no remuneration except for out-of-pocket expenses. Fiennes describes how in one operation for the group, Mason strung up a drug dealer in Bristol with parachute cord to discourage him from carrying on his antisocial trade. He was also involved in an unsuccessful operation to protect Marman from the attentions of the Clinic.

Mason now farms several thousand acres in Oxfordshire. 'I worked very occasionally for the Feather Men,' he said, and he verified those aspects of the book of which he had first-hand knowledge.

Stung by skepticism from some commentators on 'The Feather Men' (most notably from James Adams of *The Sunday Times*), David Reynolds, Deputy Managing Director of Bloomsbury, went on the attack. 'The book is indeed a thriller, but it is not fiction,' he said. 'Bloomsbury published *The Feather Men* because it contains evidence of two important matters: that the deaths of four former British soldiers were not the accidents they had been thought to be; and that there existed, and possibly still exists, a private army in this country known as the Feather Men....'

Last word goes to Sir Peter Horsley, the driver of the BMW that killed Major Michael Marman. The retired Air Marshall may be one of the few people ever to escape an assassination attempt, and what happened uncannily mirrors many aspects of the Diana crash, including the fact that Horsley, like Henri Paul, were both pilots.

As a high-powered businessman with excellent Establishment connections Horlsey would be expected to be cautious in commenting about what Fiennes disclosed. However, the details of what happened to him as he drove along the A303 in November, 1986, have made him take the story of the Clinic seriously.

In his autobiography *Sounds From Another Room* (Leo Cooper), published in 1997, he discusses the crash, the subsequent inquest into Marman's death, and the accident investigator's report. Horsley recalls that he had passed a roundabout, overtaken a horse box, and accelerated up to sixty mph when his car began to behave erratically: 'I happened to glance in the rear view mirror and saw a grey Volvo coming up fast to station itself immediately behind me. I was just about to wave it on when with alarming suddenness my BMW spun sharply to the left, and then with tires now screeching, equally sharply to the right and then back again. I was thrown from side to side as I fought to control the ever increasing gyrations....

'Out of the corner of my eye I saw the grey Volvo accelerate past me at high speed. My car had now developed a mind of its own as it swung broadside and skidded down the road. With a lurch it hit the central reservation, mounted the grass verge separating the two lanes of the highway, and crossed over into the opposite carriageway. I had just time to see a small car approaching from the opposite direction. I hit it sideways on with tremendous force. In a split-second the driver's horror-stricken face was visible and I heard his hoarse scream.'

Horsley recovered slowly from his physical injuries, but he was perplexed and distressed: 'While my wounds gradually healed, my mental anguish remained and, like a dog worrying over a bone, I went over and over the last moments before the crash. Why had my BMW suddenly gone out of control? Had it developed a mind of its own? Was it mechanical failure, a brake seizure or a burst tire? But I always returned to the essential fact that I had been traveling quite normally down a straight road when the car suddenly behaved in a violent and unexpected manner. There was no rational explanation for the unpredictability of the events thereafter.'

Horsley's bewilderment increased as it became clear his car had no mechanical faults. The police clearly believed he was to blame for the accident, and the threat of a jail sentence hung over him although a breathalyser test had proved negative. The next ordeal was the inquest, where fortunately Aubrey Allen, a land agent driving the horse box, gave important evidence. He told the Coroner's Court in Sherborne: 'The BMW was traveling normally down the center of the road in front of me when a large puff of smoke came out of the left rear side of the car. The vehicle began to swerve from side to side. The driver was obviously fighting to control the car and it then shot across the central reservation at an acute angle.'

The Coroner concluded: 'Sir Peter's vehicle was seen to snake along the A303 for some reason we may never know....' Police eventually dropped charges of careless driving, and Horsley received a call from Fiennes. 'The story of the Feather Men at least gave me a possible explanation of why my car had behaved in such a manner. The Clinic had moved on leaving behind the four dead soldiers.... Their contract had been fulfilled.'

If indeed the Horsley/Marman crash happened as Fiennes describes, the similarities with what actually befell the Mercedes driven by Henri Paul are striking. Paul swerved to the left into a pillar without apparently taking evading action. One or perhaps two cars are said to have closely shadowed the Mercedes, as did a powerful motorbike. None of these vehicles have been found.

Fiennes told the authors he had until now given little thought to the coincidences of the Diana crash. He had not been previously aware that other unidentified cars were in the close vicinity of the Mercedes. 'You need another car from which to send signals to activate the brakes or the steering,' he said. 'It now makes me wonder if there is any truth to these conspiracy theories.'

Horsley said that, after the death of Dodi and Diana, he was contacted by people curious to know his reaction. 'Of course I know nothing of what happened in Paris, but as I discovered it is technically possible to take over the control of a car by remote control, and people should be aware that there are groups around capable of doing such terrible things. In the Diana incident there appears to have been another car around, Fiat Uno.'

None of the stories in this chapter provide any proof that the Mercedes conveying Diana and Dodi was in some way tampered with by some group bent on mischief. However, they show that such a notion must not be disregarded. The authorities may try to reassure the public that nothing sinister occurred on August 31, 1997, but those same authorities are well aware that highly professional assassins operate around the world, sometimes with official sanction and with formidable resources.

The public need, however, have no doubt that terrible inventions are used by security organizations. The Russians are said to have devised a piece of portable equipment to project a deadly beam at a victim. A leaked document published in Moscow described the Genotron, first built in the late 1970s. It read chillingly: 'A saucer-sized device is fixed on the breast of the agent-killer. A left wire is connected through his shirt sleeve to a button hidden in his glove. The energy pumping cycle is seven seconds. The right wire is connected to an electron ray transmitter powered by a 9V source. When it is necessary to carry out the "clean" elimination of an "inconvenient" person, the killer walks behind the target and with the help of an ultrasound aiming device zeroes in on the victim's pulsating heart and "shoots." The result is heart defibrillation and multiple ruptures of heart tissue.'

Giorgi Markov, the Bulgarian dissident, died after being stuck in the leg by a high-tech umbrella designed to shoot a microscopic pellet of deadly poison. Only the most diligent of pathologists would have found the evidence. Contrary to its intentions, the Bulgarian regime was found out, but normally such a sudden death would be put down to natural causes. Drugs to mimic heart attacks, even when given in tiny quantities, are said to have been developed by a number of major powers, ostensibly to aid in developing antidotes.

It is a gruesome profession and, sad to say, South Africa was and maybe still is a leading exponent in 'wet affairs.' The African National Congress under Nelson Mandela is now in power, but it itself once fought a terrorist campaign against the racist apartheid regime using IRA-type tactics. What is interesting is how the Nationalist government responded. On the surface, it tried to put over an image of being a responsible Western-style state. Its intelligence services worked closely with the Central Intelligence Agency and the Defense Intelligence Agency in the US and with MI5 and MI6. But the reality, details of which are now leaking out, was quite different. The Nationalist government secretly planned and executed appalling acts of skulduggery.

The Truth and Reconciliation Commission, set up to give those involved a chance to confess in return for (in most cases) immunity from prosecution, has heard terrible stories of assassinations and a spate of dirty tricks operations. Most illuminating has been the trial of Colonel Eugene De Kock, convicted to 212 years on eighty-nine accounts including eight murders.

De Kock headed a secret police death squad called Vlakplaas (the name of a farm near Pretoria where the unit was based) which, on one occasion, bashed in a man's skull with a spade. Much of Vlakplaas's notorious past was exposed in 1989 by a former head, Captain Dirk Coetzee, who testified against De Kock. Coetzee's animosity to his colleague is understandable because at one time De Kock had also tried to kill him as a warning to any other policemen who might be inclined to break ranks.

The plan was ingenious and lead to tragedy as police 'technical man' and military intelligence agent Steve Bosch disclosed to the court. 'After Coetzee's revelations about hit squad activities at Vlakplaas in 1989, everything at Vlakplaas was mixed up,' Bosch said. 'We destroyed some things and carted away weaponry because we thought they might come to inspect the farm.

'We had to find out where Coetzee was. We listened to his telephones, kept his house under observation and followed his family.' Bosch said that orders then came from De Kock to prepare a parcel for Coetzee. 'I knew it had to be an explosive device because I couldn't prepare such a device on my own. I asked the technical section (of police security headquarters) for help.'

Following orders from his commander, Bosch had to buy two Walkman personal tape players and two music tapes. These were then sent to the security police's Rebecca Street branch in Pretoria where there was printing press and a mechanical and technical section. The mechanical section installed secret compartments in cars and built cameras into suitcases, and the electronic engineers provided photographic and video equipment and bugging devices. After both Walkmans had been adapted, Bosch was told to buy a sheep's head. He couldn't find one. 'Instead I bought a pig's head,' Bosch explained. He said explosives had been placed in the earpieces of the headphones. The wire from the tape player set these off when the tape player was switched on.

'We tried it on the pig's head and I told Col. De Kock it worked very well.'

The court heard that in May, 1990, the remaining cassette machine was put inside a padded envelope marked 'Evidence Hit Squads,' with tapes of Neil Diamond—Coetzee's favorite singer. It was posted to an address to where Coetzee had been traced in Lusaka, but then the plan went wrong. There was excess postage on the parcel when it arrived and Coetzee did not pick it up. It was therefore returned to sender. The name given on the packet was Bheki Mlangeni, a Johannesburg lawyer.

Tragically, Mlangeni was totally unaware that his name and address had been put on the pack. He tried on the headphones and the device blew off his head. The South African intelligence services had killed the wrong man.

Much is written about how much South Africa has changed since those dark days, but stories still circulate about how the high-tech 'backroom boys' are still at work, producing to order for those who require their services, which includes foreign governments. Such allegations will seem highly improbable to many readers, but an informant in Johannesburg produced a disturbing glossy leaflet to indicate that the group, which had gone 'private,' was still in action. It bore no company name, address, or phone number but advertised a 'Sniper Event Recording System.' Photographs show a sniper's rifle with a telescopic sight to which has been added a tiny video camera and a transmitter. The blurb begins: 'This unique system will ensure positive identification and visual recording of hostile and illegal activities. High-quality images can be transmitted to a command station or can be recorded on the spot. This recording system can be fitted on a sniper's standard telescope....'

We were told this device was intended for hired killers, like the Clinic, who need to provide their paymasters with proof they have done a good job. We heard from the informant that the same laboratory was making brief case bombs and equipment to cause car crashes in such a manner that they looked like accidents. 'They make the very best,' said the informant, 'and they are not very fussy about who they deal with.'

He then drew our attention to a mysterious car crash that occurred near Johannesburg in October, 1993. The vehicle was a powerful Mercedes 500 SE, driven by company director Kobus Du Preez with two passengers. As it progressed along a road known as the Golden Highway, the vehicle suddenly went out of control, leaped off the road and into the air. It demolished a tree before burying itself in the ground, killing all the occupants. One witness said there was liquid coming from the exhaust. 'As it fell on the grass, it was so hot that the grass was smoldering.'

Du Preez had been secretly dealing in nuclear materials, but perfunctory police enquiries concluded the crash was an accident. Not so, said the informant, a former agent in the security services who said he had direct knowledge of the incident. He said the car had been 'doctored' with a device that attached to the car's exhaust system, feeding carbon monoxide into the passenger compartment and making passengers comatose.

The idea the South African regime set up companies for such purposes seems incredible, but in June, 1998 more came out. At the Truth and Reconciliation Commission hearing a former military biological engineer testified that he had helped establish ten private front companies to produce biological and chemical weapons and to 'make to order' a variety of devices, including screwdrivers with an injectable poison in the handle, poison-tipped walking sticks, and all sorts bombs hidden in objects like packets of washing powder.

The witness, Dr. Jan Lourens, said the operation was called Project Coast, and experiments were initially carried out on baboons. 'I was never told what (the devices) were for,' said Lourens, 'but it was quite obvious ... I was never under any illusion that it was for any purpose other than assassinating human beings.'

Diana's last journey was so short there would be little time to tamper with the car or for such as a poison gas device to take effect. Nevertheless, it has been recently revealed that a high level of carbon monoxide was found in Henri Paul, her chauffeur's, blood. There is no adequate explanation for this.

Chapter Nine

Chaos and Confusion

As the screech of ripping metal and shattering glass was dying down, the paparazzi were on the scene of the crash within seconds. And thankfully, not only the paparazzi arrived but others from not far away who were more interested in helping the victims than cashing in on the tragedy.

Only one of the paparazzi, including both those who stayed at the scene and those who departed before the arrival of the police, made any effort to bring help to the dead and dying. And after a single failed attempt he gave up. So the task of calling in police and rescue services fell to other witnesses, a number of whom made their calls almost within seconds.

A young lady identified as Gaelle, who together with her boyfriend had witnessed the crash from the eastbound lane, stopped outside the tunnel and went to halt vehicles on the other side of the road traveling into the tunnel.

From one of these she borrowed a mobile phone and called the 'sapeurs-pompiers,' a military-controlled fire brigade unit especially equipped to tackle major road crashes, also with state-of-the-art ambulances.

At about the same time, a man in a nearby apartment heard the terrible sounds of the crash and made an immediate call to the SAMU, a civilian emergency medical service which operates around the clock in cooperation with the state-run hospitals and whose ambulances have on-board intensive care facilities. The crew of each mobile SAMU unit includes a doctor specializing in emergency medicine.

In any event, the first doctor to arrive at the scene was Frederic Mailliez who works with S.O.S. Médecins, a private medical service. Driving eastwards on his way home, he was in the tunnel within a minute of the crash, smoke and steam still in the air and the horn blaring. After investigating the crashed vehicle, Mailliez returned to his car and telephoned emergency units before going back to help the victims with a respirator.

In an article for *Impact Quotidieni,* a newspaper for doctors, Dr. Mailliez describes how he assisted the Princess, who appeared to him to be in the better condition than anyone else in the car: 'I helped her to breathe with a mask and I attempted to liberate the upper respiratory passage by bending her head back slightly. I sought to unblock the trachea and prevent the tongue from blocking the oro-pharynx. She seemed to be a bit more agitated, thus more reactive, once she was able to breath better.'

Later controversy surrounding reports that the Princess had spoken after the crash, principally from the Al Fayed camp, started with Dr. Mailliez. In the interview with *Impact Quotidiendi* and also on a CNN television show he said that the Princess spoke nothing decipherable. 'She was semiconscious, muttering, but never saying anything precise,' he said.

But a report in the *Times of London* quoted him as saying: 'She kept saying how much she hurt as I put a resuscitation mask over her mouth,' and 'I'm in pain,' and 'Oh God! I can't stand this.' In a call the next day to Associated Press the doctor denied that she had ever spoken of her pain, but the reporter on the *Times* stood by his story, refusing to publish any correction. It is an interesting episode and must throw doubt on whether it was possible for the Princess to speak to a nurse when she eventually arrived at the hospital, as reported by Mohammed Al Fayed.

The first two policemen arrived in the tunnel within five minutes to discover a chaotic scene. One of them, officer Lino Gagliardone, in a report dated August 31 said, 'We ... observed a Mercedes license plate number 688 LTV 75 with a severely damaged front end lying across the roadway facing the opposite direction, as well as a large number of people, mainly photographers, who were shooting pictures of the right rear of the vehicle, whose door was open.'

Later in the report, Officer Gagliardone lapses into the present tense, saying: 'Officer Sebastien Dorzee rushes to the site, trying to move back some photographers who put up resistance. They are virulent, pushy, and continue to take photos, intentionally preventing [him] from aiding the victim, one of them declaring [as noted earlier] while pushing the officer back, "You piss me off, let me do my work: in Sarejevo the cops let us work. You should go get shot at and you'll see what it's like."

'I observe that the occupants of the vehicle are in a very grave state. I immediately repeat the call for aid and request police reinforcements, being unable to contain the photographers and passers-by.... The first vehicle of the firemen's emergency unit arrives, begins treating victims, asks officer Dorzee to try to keep the right rear passenger awake by talking to her and tapping on her cheek, and also asks me to hold up the head of the front-right passenger. Very quickly reinforcements from the sapeurs-pompiers and SAMU arrive to assist the medical units already present.'

It is interesting to compare this report with one which might be expected from a British policeman. It is jumbled and lacks any standard form, and it is unlikely that a London officer would ever consider submitting it in that form. To be fair, it is necessary to take into account the extraordinary events of the night and the tangle of emotions affecting the officer.

His colleague, Officer Dorzee, reported in a very similar vein when he was interviewed the same night, also commenting on the aggressive behavior of the photographers. His perception of the condition of the victims is very similar to that of Dr. Mailliez. It is noteworthy that the police found the press far more belligerent than he has suggested.

Photographs taken that night show that it wasn't only the paparazzi crowding around the car. There were also a bunch of rubber-neckers on the scene, with at least one picture showing one of these almost inside the car. Others revealed some in the crowd snapping away with amateur cameras. At a very early stage, a professional crew with a video camera turned up in a party of ten or more photographers and started shooting film. These people and their film have not been discovered.

It took nearly ten minutes before the first sapeurs-pompiers' unit was on the scene with an ambulance and a technical support vehicle, and nearly as long again for the first ambulance to arrive from the SAMU. Eventually the organization had three ambulances in the tunnel, each one with a doctor and a nurse on board.

First the doctors fought to save the victims while they were trapped in the vehicle and later the sapeurs-pompiers' used specialist equipment to cut the roof off the Mercedes, and the victims were laid out on stretchers in the roadway. The medical rescue continued until they could be moved into the ambulances. Henri Paul had died immediately, while Dodi was showing no signs of life.

After intensive medical efforts had clearly failed he was officially declared dead at 1:45 A.M. Trevor Rees-Jones was alive but suffering from terrible injuries, with the bottom half of his face ripped off and his tongue partially severed. Additionally, he had serious chest and head injuries and a broken right wrist.

Diana, Princess of Wales, was assessed as being in a grave condition but appeared to have the least injuries. There were multiple fractures of the right arm, head injuries, and many cuts and abrasions—but no evidence at this stage of the internal injuries of which she would eventually die. Work started immediately in the tunnel to resuscitate her. She was reported to be in a Class 1 coma by a SAMU doctor, a designation whereby the patient is semiconscious and can make sounds without being able to speak.

Diana's blood pressure was dangerously low and it was the doctors' opinion that her condition should be stabilized before she was moved. In all, it was well over an hour after the crash before the ambulance moved away to take her to the hospital. She was not taken to the nearest, just across the Seine, as it was decided the best facilities available were at the Pitié-Salpêtrière hospital, where the capital's finest specialists were prepped-up and waiting in the operating room for her arrival.

Ordered by the doctors to travel slowly, the ambulance took forty agonizing minutes to travel the four miles (6.4 km) to the hospital and it did not arrive until 2.05 A.M., a whole hour and forty minutes after the crash. At a normal speed at that hour of the morning this is a journey which would ordinarily take less than ten minutes, and accusations were later made about the decision to move the patient so painstakingly.

Once at the hospital, Diana was rushed straight to the operating room where her serious condition persuaded the doctors that they had to operate immediately. The doctors involved were Professor Jean-Pierre Benazet, head of emergency surgery; Dr. Pierre Coriat, responsible for the anaesthesiology-intensive care department; Professor Alain Pavie, a leading cardiovascular surgeon; and the duty physician Professor Bruno Riou, an anesthesiologist.

The initial diagnoses noted by Professor Riou was that 'she suffered from very grave thoracic hemorrhaging, quickly followed by cardiac arrest.' Surgery rapidly established that the internal bleeding was coming from a tear in her left pulmonary vein, the vessel that carries oxygenated blood from the left lung into the atrium chamber of the heart.

Her lungs were flooded with blood, and she was unable to breathe without the assistance of a heart-lung machine. As a result of this internal bleeding, her major organs had been starved of oxygen and essential fluids with the result that she suffered a massive heart attack. As the ruptured blood vessel was repaired by one surgeon, the Princess was administered drugs and electric shock treatments, and for nearly two hours the other doctors massaged her heart with their hands.

As the world was shortly to learn, Diana's heart never flickered into life. Despite the almost two hours of unrelenting effort by the doctors the world's 'Queen of Hearts' was officially declared dead at 4 A.M. on August 31. The official report from the French Medical Examiner gave the cause of death as 'internal hemorrhaging due to a major chest trauma and phenomenon of deceleration which caused a rupture of the left pulmonary vein.'

Subsequent reports suggest that her life would have been saved if only she had been taken to hospital more rapidly. The French quite rightly vigorously defend their procedures for emergency treatment, claiming that they are among the most sophisticated in the world. Trevor Rees-Jones was taken to the same hospital in the same manner as the Princess, arriving some time after the ambulance with the Princess, and there has been nothing but praise for his treatment both during the trauma stage and the later reconstruction of his face.

But what about all the politicians and various 'important' people who gathered, adding to the turmoil in the tunnel under the Pont de L'Alma that night? Should they have been there, and were they responsible for unnecessary delays? Reports in the French and German press (*Bild* and *Paris-Match*) have been strongly critical of all the VIPs who thought it necessary to attend the scene.

When the report of the crash first filtered through, the fire service informed the Paris police chief Philippe Massoni as he was about to go to bed in his official apartment on the boulevard du Palais. Stopping only to telephone the French Minister for Internal Affairs, Jean-Pierre Chevenement, he rushed to the tunnel and was quickly joined there by the Minister. Then more officials arrived. There was Patrick Riou, Director of the Judiciary Police, and investigator Martine Monteil from the Paris crime squad.

It has been alleged that the emergency recovery might well have gone ahead more rapidly without the presence of all these officials, trying to decide levels of responsibility and who should take control. And all the time responsibility was being passed higher up the line. Minister Jean-Pierre Chevenement was constantly on the mobile phone. The Prime Minister Lionel Jospin was informed in Rochefort.

A search was also going on for the President, Jacques Chirac, but meanwhile there was chaos at the scene. It was not until Patrick Riou, director of the Paris Judiciary Police, arrived and later, Deputy Procurer Maud Coujard on her motorbike, that decisions were finally taken. At this stage, the immediate autopsy of the chauffeur was organized, and officers started to take statements from witnesses, confiscated the Mercedes, and ordered the total barricade of the accident scene by two brigades of the CRS.

Evidence from the French press suggests that controversy is still rife in the French capital about what happened that evening. It has been suggested that Professor Jean-Pierre Benazet, the head of emergency surgery, was reluctant to attend the press conference when the death of the Princess was announced by Professor Riou, senior physician and Jean-Pierre Chevenement, the Minister for Internal Affairs.

Having been declared dead at the scene of the crash, Dodi and Henri Paul were taken directly to the Paris morgue (the Institut Médico Legal) on the right bank of the Seine near the Austerlitz Bridge. By a macabre coincidence, Dodi's coffin was later being carried out as that containing the Princess arrived; it was the closest the couple were to be ever again.

No autopsy was conducted on either of them in France. In Dodi's case, an external body examination was all that was considered necessary. He had not been the driver of the vehicle and therefore could not have been responsible for the crash.

In the Princess' case, the same argument applied—plus, such an act was considered unthinkable given who she was. Preparations to gain permission for the bodies of both Dodi and the Princess to be returned to Britain became frantic, with intense diplomatic effort necessary to overcome the sluggishness of French officialdom. In reality, there was never going to be a problem so far as the body of Diana, Princess of Wales, was concerned, but time was of the essence to the family of

Dodi, as under Islamic law burial is necessary within twenty-four hours.

The lack of diplomatic or royal status created greater problems, and Mohammed Al Fayed particularly wanted his son to be buried on English soil. In any event, both bodies were back in Britain by Sunday. Dodi's body was transported in the Harrods helicopter, while Diana was brought home under the full pomp of state, flown with full honors by the Royal Air Force and attended by Prince Charles and Diana's sisters.

Chapter Ten

Wild Thoughts

Within minutes of the crash in the Pont de L'Alma underpass on August 31, 1997, the Internet was buzzing with reports of the death of the Princess and her Arab lover. Internet sites about the Princess as an individual and on her and Dodi as a couple already existed, but in the hours following the news breaking there was a frenzy of activity. Barely six hours after the crash, at 6:27 A.M., a new site entitled *Princess Diana Dead, Will Charles Rule?* appeared, and some thirteen minutes later a sharp Australian anticipated a new growth industry with the creation of *The First Diana Conspiracy Site.*

So it took just six hours and fifteen minutes for the conspiracy theories to start. Twelve hours after news of the crash filtered into a stunned world consciousness, a news agency check on the Web server Alta Vista discovered nearly 100 new or updated contributions—the 'anoraks' never sleep!

These entries, mostly concentrating on the conspiracy theme, were to multiply over the next few days. Seemingly breeding, one off the other, the theories rapidly grew in originality and wildness. One contributor thought the villain of the piece must be British comic Eddie Large, who, it was suggested, needed to draw tabloid press attention away from a 'road rage' conviction!

Even *Interflora* got a dishonorable mention on the basis that it would be good for business (which, judging by the floral tributes outside Kensington Palace in the days after the crash, proved to be a reasonable forecast on some level at least), while yet another contributor thought Dodi's ex-girlfriend Kelly Fisher might have been behind the whole event.

Continuing the good work, a lady from Bilbao thought an Arab Terror-Commando group was probably responsible.

To give some measure of the fever, a 'Diana conspiracy' Internet search carried out some three months after the event discovered over 31,000 entries, with most of the ideas posed being completely off the wall.

There is nothing new about conspiracy theories. As a phenomenon, they have been flourishing worldwide since the death of President Kennedy, the bedrock of the whole industry. Since that seminal event, the premature death of just about every public figure, whether from the ranks of politics, showbusiness, or royalty, has engendered its own plot or 'something-gate,' and mostly the argument has been presented that the 'order to kill' must have emanated from government or its agents, or possibly out-of-control government hit-men.

As an alternative culprit, theorists have often pointed to big business and particularly the multinational military/industrial complex. So the suicide of Marilyn Monroe, the car crash which killed Princess Grace, and the shootings of American civil rights leader Martin Luther King and also Senator Robert Kennedy have all been attributed to organized and well-funded murder squads.

In an increasingly cynical world, it has become a knee-jerk reaction to attribute these deaths to murder, dressed up to look like something totally different. Media coverage given to

conspiracies, coupled with the easy acceptance in many countries of elimination by murder, has led to the popular perception that this is one way in which control is exerted by major
power groups over individuals who are perceived to be out of
control or endangering the interests of particular, powerful
organizations. In the mythology of 'conspiracy,' it now seems
inevitable that 'zig-zagging white car' will stand alongside the
'grassy knoll' and 'Roswell, New Mexico' as symbols of the
almost cosmic power of conspirators.

Prior to the deaths of Diana, Princess of Wales and Dodi
Fayed, those organizations or individuals which inspired the
most active conspiracy theories were reasonably easy to
define. In virtually all the earlier situations it was simple to
identify a particular beneficiary or reason for a conspiracy.
Everyone knew and, if they didn't, the media would soon tell
them who would have wanted Marilyn Monroe and President
Kennedy, for example, eliminated and why.

All the necessary circumstances for a conspiracy theory
came together in the crash in the Pont de L'Alma underpass.
The Princess was deeply distrusted by the Royal Family and
had been publicly branded a 'loose cannon' by its closest advisors. She had offended the international arms industry with a
potent campaign against land mines and, even worse, she was
nominated for a Nobel Peace Prize—which would have raised
the stakes against the military/industrial complex to a new and
higher level.

The British Establishment was horrified that a wealthy Arab
playboy could become the stepfather of Princes William and
Harry, second and third in line to the British throne. Rumors
were already widespread in the higher echelons of British society that the Princess was pregnant, and further complexities
for the Royal Family were forecast with the possibility of a

Muslim half-brother for the Princes. And worse yet, should the Princess have decided to marry Dodi Fayed and convert to Islam, as her friend Jemima Goldsmith had done following her marriage to cricketer-turned-politician Imran Khan, it could have had repercussions for the relationship between Church and State.

One fear was that if their mother converted, the Princes might be persuaded to follow suit, which would render them ineligible to inherit the crown or, should the conversion come after a coronation, abdication would be required. Such an upheaval, however unlikely, would be profoundly unsettling for the monarchy and would open the doors for the advocates of republicanism to press their arguments to an increasingly receptive public.

Exaggerated as it may seem, the relationship between the 'wayward flower' of the British aristocracy and the Arab heir was seen as a very real threat to the Crown, although, in any event, the death of the Princess has apparently since initiated a stronger relationship between Crown and Country. There was yet another strand in the whole conspiracy theory: the romance was also perceived in Israel as a threat to its interests, possibly moving the balance of world opinion more favorably in the direction of Arab culture and consequently against Israeli interests.

Within each of these three strands, the British Establishment, the military/industrial complex, and the Israeli State, there were both the expertise and the money to mount any operation necessary to eliminate 'the problem.' Throw in (for good measure) the fact that many in the Arab world took the British Establishment's distaste surrounding the Diana-Dodi relationship as a direct racial insult, then it is easy to understand why conspiracy theories found both early strong expression and a ready acceptance in the Middle East.

So it was no surprise when the Arab media, particularly in Egypt, the early home of the Fayed family, erupted with conspiracy mania. For weeks prior, the newspapers, TV, and radio had been reporting the developing romance with breathless excitement. The possibility of a marriage was seen as the precursor to an explosion of world influence for the whole region, bringing enhanced prestige and respectability, just as the Israelis feared.

In this fevered atmosphere, the finality of the deaths was a crushing blow, a setback to the ambitions of the State, hence quickly perceived as almost a personal insult. Against this background, it was not a great intellectual leap to believe that if the romance had challenged some balance of international power then the 'accident' must have been planned and carried out with official authority, by rogue officials without authority, or by some other international force.

So many of the events which took place in Paris in the hours leading up to the crash and during the moments it was taking place remain unexplained that even the most agnostic of observers cannot dismiss the possibility of a planned event. The Princess herself had often expressed fears for her safety and had suggested that even her own helicopter was a dangerous place for somebody who had compromised her 'popularity' with so many vested interests. It has been reported through her office in St James' Palace, London, that she received death threats on a daily basis. Both the Princess and her sons had to undertake a security training test with the S.A.S. twice a year.

In truth, the choice of a car crash is one of the *less* believable aspects of a conspiracy theory. It would have been easier to eliminate the Princess and Dodi (or just one or the other—

the target for a possible assassination has not been established) in far more controllable conditions. It would surely have been far more practical to blow up one of the Fayed family yachts — the technology is simple. It can be achieved far from land, out of sight of prying eyes and witnesses, and far from the annoying interference of the emergency services.

An air crash would be another effective and simple solution, especially if it could be engineered over the sea. Poisons could also be considered. But a car? That presents a barrage of problems when dealing with a family as wealthy as the Fayeds. Firstly they have a multitude of choices of vehicle, with the result that any one eventually used is likely to be the outcome of a blind lottery. Secondly, routes can be unpredictable, subject to change at the briefest of occasions.

Additionally, traffic conditions can combine to make an attack difficult, if not impossible. An underpass late at night is possibly just about the best location to suit the objectives.

In any case, with the bandwagon rolling, theories continued to proliferate. Those accused of being responsible for hatching devious plans ranged from heads of state, the Queen herself, and the Pope, to the British, American, Chinese, and Italian arms industries, and the CIA. The British Labour Party found itself named as another villain. Drug dealers also popped up on the list of likely culprits, as did Hollywood film producers, the latter on the grounds that it would later make a superb story line for a major movie! This eventually became a popular theme, especially in the US.

The Hollywood story became amplified in a number of ways. Firstly, it was suggested that Dodi's background in the film business enabled him to stage the whole event himself to enable the love-lorn couple to be secreted away to an idyllic island in the sun where they could live in peace and tranquillity. The fertile brains behind this scenario later 'improved' the scheme to include plastic surgery for the Princess so that she could return to visit her sons. This story line was even further embellished to include assistance by the Paris authorities so that there would be no leaks to the press.

'Ru Mills,' whose name developed from the term 'rumor mills,' a regular contributor to the Internet, proposed a slightly different scenario, although one that also involved a return by the Princess. Continuing the theme of British Secret Service involvement, Ru wrote, '... even within British intelligence there are factions. A rogue faction in MI6, powerless to prevent the assassination, arranged for the deaths of Lady Diana and Dodi Fayed to happen at Pont de L'Alma.'

Cleverly, it was known that a death at that historic location would not only 'send a signal,' it would eventually lead to the creation of a 'Saint Diana.' In Roman paganism, Diana is 'Queen of Heaven,' a triple goddess. 'Al-mah,' in mideast language, means 'moon goddess.' One aspect of the Roman triple-goddess is the 'lunar virgin.' The 'al-mahs' served as maidens of Diana, the lunar virgin.

Having 'established' the historical and religious authentication for the victim and the place of the assassination, Ru Mill then postulates the full sanctification of the Princess as well as how it would be achieved. 'Before too long,' she writes, 'Project Blue Beam holographic imaging will be used to create 'miraculous appearances' of Lady Diana. Children at various locations will be randomly selected to witness 'saintly apparitions.' She goes on:

'These will claim that Diana has given them healing powers—and what is more, these children will be able to heal. Locations of these "miraculous appearances" will become known as places of healing and sacred shrines. "Saint Diana's" two children, William and Harry, will become akin to two living Jesus Christs, walking the earth. It will be the start of "the new religion." Who controls the new religion controls the world.'

So there we have it. The plot has nothing to do with eliminating an embarrassment to the Crown and Government: the crash was historically preordained to create the new religion!

Yet another similar theme was postulated by Anita Sands, an enthusiastic contributor to the Internet conspiracy files. Believing the two deaths were all in the stars, she tracked the crash astrologically in a long and complicated interpretation titled *Uranus Romances: Fire Too Hot to Cool Down*. In Sands' article it would seem that everything was predictable through the powers of astrology, except apparently the capacity to write it prior to the event.

In Part Four of Sherman Skolnick's extensive analysis of the events in Paris entitled *UK, French, Journalists Confide: Princess Diana was Assassinated*, Skolnick goes into great detail on the 'D' Notice system in Britain whereby Government has some control over the stories published in the media. It is Skolnick's proposition that the truth of the 'assassination' has not been exposed in the British press because of the existence of a secret ban.

Skolnick claims that the 'D' Notice is part of the Official Secrets Act, and not only allows the Government to forbid the publication of particular stories but also permits the authorities to '... immediately seize and close down any printing plant that is in the process of printing such a story, any radio station, or any radio or TV transmitter involved in disseminating a given story. They are immediately seized by the London government, closed down, and the publisher, the editor, and the key personnel (including the writer of the story) are immediately put under arrest.'

Skolnick continues, 'And the worst part of it is, the rest of the media is not even allowed to mention that these people have been arrested and their publishing and transmitting facilities seized.' In other words, it is forbidden to discuss the 'D' Notice and also forbidden to discuss the technical operation of the Official Secrets Act. So, there is censorship regarding the instruments of censorship.

It is an interesting scenario, but totally wrong. The 'D' Notice is a voluntary code without any legal backing, and editors are usually given a full briefing on the background and reason for a 'D' Notice and why it is necessary. None has been issued on any matter to do with the Diana crash.

If all this is not fanciful enough, here are a few more stories from the Internet Conspiracy files: It was carried out to allow Prince Charles to marry Camilla Parker-Bowles. It was to prevent a civil war between any child of Di and Dodi and the Princes William and Harry. It was a revenge attack by a business rival of Mohammed Al Fayed. It was the British Conservative Party avenging the cash-for-questions scandal in which Mr. Al Fayed gave money to various MPs, including Neil Hamilton, to ask questions in Parliament, and then leaked the story to the press at the time of the General Election in 1997.

Foreign governments were anxious not to be left out. In Libya, the head of state Colonel Muammar Ghaddafi, who claims that Mohammed Al Fayed hails from Libyan stock, joined in allegations that the British and French secret services arranged the accident because they were annoyed that a British Princess might marry an Arab.

Egypt has been anxious to stake its claim to the conspiracy market. Egyptian publishers have already pumped out several books on the flimsy claim that the crash was instigated by

Buckingham Palace. Now a well-known Egyptian film-maker, Khairy Beshara is planning a plot along similar lines. The *Washington Post*'s correspondent John Lancaster commented: 'Egypt's susceptibility to conspiracy theories is not entirely without foundation. The history of the Middle East is rife with real-life conspiracies, from the palace intrigues of the Ottoman empire to Israel's botched attempt ... to assassinate a Hamas leader in Jordan by injecting him with an exotic poison.

'Many Egyptians, moreover, were miffed by the refusal of their former colonial ruler to grant citizenship to Dodi's father, Mohammed Al Fayed, the owner of Harrods department store in London. They also felt slighted by Western media reports that treated the death of his son as little more than a footnote to that of Diana.

'Reports of a plot to kill Dodi and Diana surfaced within days of the accident.... That theme has been embellished by a flood of quickie books like Ilham Sharshar's *Diana, a Princess Killed by Love,* now in its third printing. "No matter what the results of the investigations, there are a lot of doubts that it was an accident," Sharshar wrote darkly. "It was very obvious, even to the British, that there are those who see their deaths as a happy ending."

'"Who killed her?" asked a competing account, *Diana's Conversion to Islam,* according to a partial translation in the English-language newspaper *al-Ahram Weekly.* "British intelligence? Israeli intelligence? Or both? We believe that Diana's conversion to Islam was the reason she was killed.... Hadn't she said she was going to shock the world?"'

Lancaster's article closes with the thought: 'Some Egyptian commentators have mocked their countrymen's penchant for believing the worst. The *al-Ahram Weekly,* for example, dryly comments on the failure of one sensation-mongering author to "implicate the French company that first built the tunnel in the murder."'

It is clearly a mad world out there, although it has to be said that some of these conspiracy theorists at least had more obvious candidates than Interflora and Eddie Large. Having worked out who stood to benefit from the deaths of Di and Dodi, it was only a short step for the theorists to discuss the mechanics of each respective operation.

Already under suspicion for causing the accident by dangerous driving, the paparazzi now found themselves targets of Internet stories suggesting that at least one of them must have been a professional killer. Other stories came to the different conclusion that the Fayed's security staff were themselves in the pay of more sinister forces and had actively participated in causing the crash. A further bizarre idea moved along the lines of *The Manchurian Candidate,* whereby systematic brainwashing had programmed one of the occupants of the car, presumably with the exception of the Princess, to engineer the crash.

Without citing all the bizarre imaginings of weirdos on the Internet, the selection discussed here gives some idea of the madness in the medium. The Internet has made it possible for rumors that once would have taken months, or even years, to filter around the world to become common currency within just days.

It is also reasonable to add that the failure of the French investigators to keep the press and media informed of the progress of their inquiries, plus the inordinate length of time they have been taking, has allowed the rumor-mongers to run wild. If the vast majority of the conspiracy theories can be rejected totally out of hand, it is nevertheless true that at least some require further investigation.

Chapter Eleven

Driven to Disaster

N o criticism has been made of any erratic driving by Henri Paul as he set out from the Ritz Hotel with his VIP passengers. The short distance was covered in a sensible manner, through the narrow streets behind the Ritz to the spacious Place de la Concorde (the Parisian equivalent to Hyde Park Corner). In the center of the square is an Egyptian obelisk, the twin of London's Cleopatra's Needle, and traffic negotiating this busy route has to pass through a number of traffic lights around the periphery to reach any of the roads radiating off.

The photographers pursuing the Mercedes and other witnesses in the Place easily caught up with Paul at a red light outside the Hotel Crillon. Some of the photographers seized the opportunity to take a couple of flash pictures, and this may have riled Paul. The instant the lights changed, he put his foot down hard on the accelerator and sped up the last leg of the square, past the entrance to the Avenue des Champs-Elysées; then he turned right down the sloping approach-road to the west-bound expressway—the Cours la Reine.

The photographers say that by this point in the journey he was accelerating fast up to motorway speeds and he soon left them far behind. The expressway is one of Paris' fastest roads, but there is a fifty-kilometer-per-hour speed limit (thirty-one mph), which is widely disregarded. The road is built partly on land reclaimed from the River Seine, which it follows for long distances. The architects built tunnels to negotiate the many bridges (Ponts) joining the left and right banks, and so the road frequently curves with a far more variable gradient and sharper camber than a proper motorway or autoroute.

The initial stretch taken by Paul beneath the Pont Alexandre III and then the Pont Des Invalides is an almost straight part of the expressway. The Mercedes would have no difficulty reaching more than 112 kph (seventy mph) and with little risk to the occupants at that time of night, when traffic was light. However, the next stretch to the Pont de L'Alma tunnel veers to the left, as does the Seine, and the road curves and dips down towards the tunnel entrance. It is at this point that Paul's driving skills would have been more thoroughly tested.

He must have driven along the road hundreds of times before, but there is one slight obstacle of which he might not have been aware. Just before the entrance is a slight hollow across the road, creating, it is argued, a hazard for very fast-moving traffic. A car hitting this dip at high speed might lose traction for a split second, and this might cause the steering of the Mercedes to be less responsive.

If, as is possible, Paul tried to overtake a slower-moving vehicle in the right lane at just this moment, he might have gone into a skid. One must, however, bear in mind that the Mercedes was heavily laden, altogether more than two tons, and was equipped with multifarious safety systems including ABS braking. These top-of-the-line vehicles are designed to remain glued to the road surface under much more testing conditions, including wet. It was a fine evening at the time.

Those witnesses who indicated they believed that the Mercedes struck an unidentified car with a glancing blow seem to be corroborated by debris found on the road just inside the tunnel entrance. The tunnel is typical of many on British motorways; a series of strip lights illuminate each sidewall, and there are pillars supporting the roof along a central reservation between the dual carriageways.

Unlike British, US, and most French motorways, there were no crash barriers dividing the two carriageways (and there were still none as this book went to press in summer, 1998—only a raised curb). It was between pillars 'two' and 'five' that pieces of clear and red glass and fragments of a mirror were subsequently found, only some of it from the Mercedes.

Around this point there is a nineteen-meter single skid mark in the fast lane, curving towards the central reservation and then back again. If it was made by the Mercedes, it would indicate that its left-side wheels first skidded to the left before the driver recovered control and skidded back towards the center of the two-lane roadway. There is speculation therefore that Paul may have been negotiating his car with some difficulty around another that was occupying the right-hand (slow) lane.

For a further stretch, there is an absence of wheel markings on the roadway and then there are two parallel skid marks thirty-two meters long, curving to the right directly towards the central reservation and the point of impact. The car hit pillar 'thirteen' head on, almost midway between its front headlights. It then rebounded, turning round a full 180 degrees, but not turning over, and finally coming to a halt on the other side of the carriageway against the near sidewall of the tunnel. There is little doubt the skid marks show the car was braking hard and trying to slow down as it went out of control.

A rear-view mirror and some indicator glass were found on the eastbound carriage, but the interest of the investigators focused on the earlier debris near the tunnel entrance. Apart from fragments that came from the Mercedes, and which could have been thrown back along the road after it hit the pillar, there was part of the taillight of a Fiat Uno, narrowed down to one of 10,000 sold in France and still in use. Further detective work on specks of paint on the Mercedes bodywork led forensic chemists to conclude that the composition was a type marketed as Bianco Corfu.

This evidence led to the interesting but still tenuous theory that the Mercedes had struck a Fiat Uno a glancing blow as it entered the tunnel. That it was apparently a white car, rather than dark in color as witnesses claim, has not been resolved. That the Uno was not smashed up by the impact but was capable of carrying on and disappearing into thin air, is yet another puzzle.

With little else to go on, the hunt was on for one of 10,000 white Fiat Unos, but whether such an enormous exercise was worth the effort depended on one further and possibly flawed assumption. The paint shade found on the Mercedes, known as Bianco Corfu, had been used on no less than ten different models of car in recent years. If, as is possible, the pieces of taillight were the result of an earlier crash in the tunnel, the famous Fiat Uno could be illusory, and certainly explain why no such car or its driver has been tracked down.

Jean Pietri, a consulting engineer for Peugeot and Citroen, is a major proponent of the theory that the Mercedes skidded out of control as it tried to overtake another vehicle. Employed by Thomas Sancton and Scott MacLeod, authors of the book *Death of a Princess,* Pietri used the term 'trampoline effect' to describe the motion of the Mercedes outside the tunnel entrance when it arrived at the hollow in the roadway. He said that the car would lose traction and, if it tried to steer around another vehicle at that point, it would likely have gone into a skid.

He believes that Paul managed to bring the car back towards the center of the roadway, but his path ahead was still impeded by the other vehicle—the Fiat Uno. Pietri concludes that finding the Fiat in its way, the Mercedes suddenly veered to the left. Its front wing hit the rear left corner of the Fiat, breaking the Mercedes' headlight and the Fiat's taillight, hence the debris. The two cars now brushed alongside each other, causing the paint scrapes on the Mercedes, before Paul pulled his car free.

In his report, Pietri reasons that the Mercedes was still traveling at a speed of well over sixty mph (ninety-seven kph)at this point. He believes Paul's way back to the right-hand (slow) lane was still impeded by the Fiat, which may have accelerated to keep pace. Further ahead, the Citroen BX of Mohammed M. was a further obstacle. 'The driver of the Mercedes then executes a second countermaneuver towards the left to avoid, at all costs, spinning into the right lane,' says Pietri. He concludes that moving the steering wheel to the left put the Mercedes into a second skid and led to the car ramming into pillar 'thirteen.'

It is a plausible theory in that it welds together many fragments of evidence, but it is clearly founded on various assumptions. From his testimony, Mohammed M. does not appear to have seen anything of the Fiat or any other second car, nor does his girlfriend mention one. To explain why Paul could not easily overtake the Uno, Pietri surmises that the Fiat might have been a high-powered version, capable of keeping pace with the Mercedes. The truth is that no one knows for certain, and the failure to identify any car in the right lane as the Mercedes entered the tunnel is clearly a big problem. As already stated, none of the witnesses to the actual crash reported seeing a white car, let alone an Uno or a high-powered one.

From pictures of the damage to the Mercedes, serious though it was, Pietri discounts stories that the car crashed at more that 120 mph (193 kph). These were partly based on reports that the Mercedes' speedometer had stuck at this reading, an impossibility as it was electronic and automatically returned to zero. He puts the speed at impact at less than sixty mph (ninety-seven kph). Richard Cuerden, head of the Accident Research Centre at the University of Birmingham in Britain, put the speed as low as forty-four mph (seventy-one kph) in an initial study, while his colleague, Professor Murray Mackay, also from Birmingham, produced the same figure as Pietri, sixty mph.

Mackay is a renowned expert on accident analysis in Britain and the United States, and he has studied the Diana crash using published material. He also visited the accident scene in order to reconstruct what, in his expert opinion, happened. 'People seeing pictures of the wreck may be surprised that the car was not traveling faster when it hit the pillar,' he said. 'The truth is that you can calculate pretty exactly from the type of damage that occurred and my figures for the speed are pretty reliable.

'From the final skid marks, you can tell it must have been doing around eighty mph (129 kph) when it entered the tunnel. It then braked down to sixty mph. You have to suspect that Henri Paul just lost it. Had he been sober it is difficult to believe the accident could have occurred in this way.' Certainly Paul was not a speed freak. His best friend, Claude Garrec, describes how he was always the first to buckle his belt (though he did not on the night of the crash) and how he had no interest in driving fast on their trips to Brittany.

Mackay said that the two parallel skid marks leading

directly to the thirteenth pillar were undoubtedly caused by the Mercedes as it braked sharply, and it is reasonable to suppose that the earlier skid mark, nearer the tunnel entrance, was also made a few seconds earlier. However, this is not completely certain. 'I have examined this mark, and it is less clearcut. It could have been made by another car on an earlier occasion. No doubt the French investigation will sort that out.'

The presence of a smaller car, of whatever type, near the tunnel entrance, and as seen by some, but not all witnesses, is crucial to the 'accident theory.' Mackay said it is far more difficult to explain why the car left such a strange pattern of skid marks if the tunnel was clear of traffic when the Mercedes sped into it. Paul was over the limit, but he drove well enough around the Place de la Concorde. Why was he not able to control the vehicle and negotiate the tunnel, or at the very least avoid such a catastrophic head-on impact? Why did he go so ridiculously fast?

Six months after the accident, another factor entered the investigators' calculations—the functioning of the airbags for the front passengers. There were none in the rear. According to the French newspaper *Le Parisien,* judge Hervé Stephan had ordered new checks to be made on the wrecked car following a detailed medical report on the injuries suffered by the occupants, particularly by Trevor Rees-Jones. He was the only occupant of the car to have been wearing a seat belt, another puzzle, and despite this and the airbag he still suffered serious head injuries.

One man who came upon the crash, and who put a call into the civilian rescue unit, SAMU, said: 'The guy in the front passenger seat was badly injured but conscious.... The lower half of his face was ripped off and hanging loose.' It seemed possible that the front passenger airbag was somehow activated seconds before the impact.

A trauma expert was quoted as saying that Rees-Jones' injuries were due to several successive shocks which took place over a period of seconds—the first being lateral, the second frontal. His injuries indicated that the car sustained an initial impact strong enough to set off the airbag. This would have protected his face, but not the right side of his head, 'which was hit by a rigid, blunt object.' There was then the major impact when the car hit pillar thirteen.

If Paul's airbag had inflated prematurely, this would clearly have caused him problems with steering the vehicle. But what set them off? A minor brush with another vehicle, as postulated by Pietri, would imply that the Mercedes' airbag system was faulty, as it is designed only to activate in the event of a serious frontal collision. There is apparently no evidence of a fault, and the system was checked only a month before the crash.

If the Mercedes hit the mystery car with more substantial force, how did the other car survive serious damage, and why did the driver fail to stop? Once again the theories—for that is all they are—are difficult to reconcile.

Henri Paul was drunk, or so the subsequent blood tests indicate, and to many readers, that will explain just about everything. Incapacitated by too much pastis, and unfamiliar with driving a big car (he normally drove a Austin Mini automatic), he went too fast, lost control, and rammed the tunnel support. Professor Mackay agreed that the amount of alcohol apparently consumed by Paul was the important factor. 'He would have had slow and inadequate responses,' he told the authors. 'All research shows that if you taken the equivalent of eight or nine shots of whisky, you are far, far more incompetent.' But one must be cautious before jumping to conclusions.

Mackay agreed that, until the mystery vehicle was found, no one could be quite sure why Paul drove so recklessly.

The Mercedes 280 is a big and heavy car but not the biggest in the Mercedes range. A 1994 model, it had a six-cylinder, 195 horsepower, 2.8 liter engine; automatic transmission; power steering; ABS anti-lock braking; and a number of other advanced features. It was designed to be both safe and easy to drive, with exceptional road-holding capacity, and although Henri Paul had not obtained a permit to drive the vehicle, there is little doubt he would have easily acquired one. After all, he had been in a Mercedes advanced driving course several times and he was a qualified pilot with good reaction times.

Mackay said: 'He was going too fast—it was a thirty-mph (forty-eight-kph) limit—but he was in a superb car. He may not have had a special license to use it, but it is an easy vehicle to drive. It would really respond to the touch of the wheel and go wherever it was steered.'

The various tests on his corpse showed blood alcohol readings of 1.87 grams per liter and 1.74 grams per liter; more than three times the French limit of 0.50 grams per liter and double the higher British limit of 0.80 grams per liter. It indicates that Paul should never have agreed to take the wheel of the car, but it does not prove beyond question that his consumption of pastis or other drinks was to blame.

One suggestion circulating in the aftermath of the crash was that the test results were made up or that Paul was somehow injected with alcohol after the event. It is a far-fetched notion without a shred of evidence. What is more intriguing is the possibility that a mistake, deliberate or otherwise, was made with the blood tests. We shall return to that later, but the fact that Paul liked a drink is not in doubt. What is much less certain is that he was an alcoholic, as we have already discussed.

Friends and relatives deny it and so does the Al Fayed camp. As we have seen, others saw him drinking two glasses of pastis immediately before leaving the Ritz. But if he was a habitual drinker, it is odd that this was not spotted in the checkup for his pilot's license only days before the crash. Dodi's security man, Trevor Rees-Jones, saw no signs of incapacity, nor did his colleague Kes Wingfield, and the video footage of Paul in the Ritz shows him to be acting quite normally. Surely, they say, his devotion to his very important clients would have caused such a meticulous character to remain sober.

There is, however, another factor that must be added to these calculations. Days after the crash it emerged that tests on Paul's blood showed traces of the antidepressant Prozac and a tranquilizer called Tiapride, alternatively known as Tiapridel. It undoubtedly helped to convince many people that Paul was utterly irresponsible and culprit number one for the killing of a beloved Princess. Many press articles advanced the view that this cocktail of pills would surely incapacitate him further, and some even argued erroneously that the drugs were a classic cocktail for the treatment of alcoholics.

The facts are less comfortable. Prozac's fame and popularity as an antidepressant is partly due to the fact that, as a modern drug, it does not hinder concentration or make people more accident prone when driving a vehicle, unlike older types of antidepressants. It might even make people drive better.

What of the tranquilizer, Tiapride? It was irrelevant. The blood tests showed 'infra-therapeutic' levels, that is, only a tiny trace—possibly from a pill taken days before. However, much more important forensic evidence was to emerge. This showed that Paul had been poisoned by carbon monoxide before the crash, a factor that received too little notice. Apart from the alcohol and traces of prescription drugs, 20.7 percent of the hemoglobin in his blood, the component carrying oxygen to all parts of the body, had been converted to 20.7 percent carboxyhemoglobin by inhalation of carbon monoxide.

This odorless gas is present in car exhausts, and it is what kills people who connect their exhaust pipe by tube to the passenger compartment and start the engine. It is also caused by faulty gas heaters, and people who smoke heavily will consume a small amount. However, the quantity consumed by Paul, who did not smoke heavily, cannot easily be explained.

Concentrations of 20 to 30 percent carbon monoxide poisoning cause headache, dizziness, and palpitations on exercise and 30 to 40 percent can cause collapse. Paul showed no such symptoms of discomfort or fatigue as the hotel video and the witnesses have testified. And how had Paul managed to absorb this quantity of gas that evening? There is said to have been none in Dodi Fayed's bloodstream, in which case it could not have been caused by the Mercedes.

Could Paul have been gassed earlier? The scenario is unlikely. His Mini, which he could have rigged up for this purpose, remained in view all evening outside the Champmesle bar. Nothing suspicious was found in his apartment, and prior to that he was driving the Range Rover, which had no obvious fault. There is one possible explanation which has enormous repercussions—that the blood test result is wrong; that they tested a blood sample of someone else. Such mistakes do occur and in the hectic atmosphere on the night of the crash it could have happened. But this is more than an issue of incompetence—for if the tests cannot be trusted, the assertion Paul was drunk falls flat. It relies almost exclusively on the measurements made of the alcohol in his blood.

Chapter Twelve

Seeing and Believing

Eyewitnesses are a frustrating species. By a mere stroke of fate they happen to be on the spot when a crime or a disaster occurs. They see the event unfolding before their very eyes. Then the information is logged in their memory cells and, in principle, they are in a position to recollect precisely what they saw. It should be a simple matter for the police or journalists to piece these stories together and present a complete jigsaw of what occurred.

But, as is well known, if a group of people are asked to recall an incident there will always be discrepancies. One witness might think they saw someone in a blue coat, whereas another may describe it as brown. They might disagree about the make of a car or the age of someone driving it. Others might make even more fundamental errors of judgment.

A recent British television advertisement showed a disheveled young man apparently attacking a passerby in the street. Viewed from a different direction it showed him clearly pushing the passerby out of the way of something falling from scaffolding. It demonstrated that both memory and people's powers of observation are fickle things.

As this book went to press, attempts were being made to untangle the conflicting stories told by about twenty people, including nine photographers and a motorbike rider who accompanied one of them, who saw the aftermath of the crash of Dodi and Diana's Mercedes. In what the French judicial system calls a general 'confrontation,' they gathered before Judge Hervé Stephan to chew over what they believe happened in the hope of producing a coherent story.

Diana's mother Frances Shand Kydd and Mohammed Al Fayed came face-to-face with the photographers they believed hounded their children to their deaths. The Harrods boss railed against them when he emerged for an afternoon break.

'If I was not in a court room, I would hang them all,' he said. 'The immorality, the inhumanity of what they did. They were like vultures around the bodies.' He also had harsh words for Diana's mother, accusing her of snobbery: 'I'm an ordinary person. I'm a working-class guy. She thinks she's the Queen of Sheba. She didn't talk to me.' But he praised Judge Hervé Stephan for being compassionate and precise: 'He uncovered many things today. Now it's in God's hands.'

Also present were Henri Paul's parents, who, like Al Fayed and Shand Kydd, had the right to attend because they are civil parties in the case. According to lawyers and witnesses, the judge interviewed each photographer one by one, asking each to describe their role that night. He then questioned them, asked other witnesses what they had seen, and allowed all the lawyers to cross-examine.

Photographer Romuald Rat was apparently questioned sharply by lawyers for Al Fayed, who tried to establish that he had pursued the Mercedes that night. 'I followed it. I did not pursue it,' Rat insisted.

Ten witnesses other than the press pack were summoned, but only eight showed up. They included the first emergency doctor on the scene, Frederic Mailliez, and the first two policemen. Lawyers said the policemen accused Rat of hindering their work. Another witness, private chauffeur Clifford Gooroovadoo, said he'd told the judge he had seen Rat and another photographer, Christian Martinez, fighting just after the accident. He said that Rat, after taking his own pictures, yelled at Martinez to stop.

The photographers were still being investigated on suspicion of manslaughter and failing to come to the aid of a person in danger. Nikolas Arsov of the Sipa photo agency called the hearing inconvenient—he was supposed to be covering the French Open tennis tournament. 'It's the fortieth time we have answered the same questions,' he said. 'It's annoying, but what can you do?'

In contrast to previous hearings, all cameras were kept outside the Palais de Justice and the gates were heavily guarded. It was revealed that tests were still being conducted on the wrecked Mercedes and these were unlikely to be finished before October 1998, further delaying the conclusion of the investigation.

By the summer of 1998, hope that the probe would answer all the puzzling discrepancies was fading. The problem facing Stephan and his team becomes obvious when one examines in more detail what people say they saw on the fateful night. They cannot even agree that another car played a role in the crash, let alone provide a coherent story about the presence of the now infamous white Fiat Uno.

Take for example, the tale of motorcyclist Eric Petel, whose recollections are uncomfortable news for those who believe the Uno may have helped cause the crash. He was driving home and was just about to enter the Pont de L'Alma tunnel when the Mercedes driven by Henri Paul sped past. One might have thought the investigators would cherish such a crucial witness. Not so. For months they believed he made up his story, though his presence at the crash was not in dispute. Now his report is regarded as being of great importance.

Petel's story is detailed and revealing: 'I saw a car in my rear-view mirrors flashing its headlamps. I moved across to let it by and it raced past even though I was doing about seventy mph. An instant later, I heard a deafening noise and saw the accident.

'The car was spinning in the road. The front was completely crushed and smoke was rising from the engine. I stopped. There were no other cars or bikes around at all and I could see all the way through the tunnel.

'The roof of the Mercedes was totally smashed in. The right-hand rear door was partly open and I looked in and saw a woman. She seemed to have been thrown forward from the back seat and had her head between the front seats.

'She had her back to me and I could just see her hair. She was wearing a jacket and trousers. I wanted to get her and the other people out. There was smoke and I thought the car might burst into flames. I reached inside and leaned the woman's head back onto the rear elbow rest.

'Blood was flowing from her right ear. I brushed hair off her face. Her eyelashes were fluttering but she hadn't opened her eyes. I asked if she was OK and she didn't answer. Only then did I realize it was Princess Diana.'

Petel says he stopped touching her, shut the car door, and decided to go for help. 'It seemed I was there for an eternity. But in fact, it was about one minute. I got back on my bike and went the wrong way up a slip road, heading for the phone box in the Place de L'Alma. I still hadn't seen a soul.

'I called the police and told them Princess Diana had been in an accident. The person at the other end laughed and told me to stop fooling around. He said, "This number is for real emergency calls. Stop wasting our time." I was very annoyed. I got back on my bike and headed for the police station in Avenue Mozart.'

According to Antoine Deguines, Petel's lawyer, he was kept waiting for twenty-five minutes, taken into a back room where the police slapped handcuffs on him. Eventually he was set free but told to follow a police car on his bike to another police station where a statement was finally taken. Without reading it, he signed the document and was then released.

'I was outraged,' Petel continued. 'They didn't seem to care about the crash.'

Petel heard nothing from the authorities until he was invited to see Hervé Stephan at the beginning of February. Deguines said he was relieved the judge was at long last taking the statement seriously. But where does that leave others' stories? Petel had seen no other vehicles. He had allegedly spent a minute with Diana, then left to phone police without seeing anyone else.

In only some respects Petel's story is corroborated by a witness called Mohammed M. who was driving west through the tunnel with his girlfriend Souad ahead of the crash. Mohammed has reportedly said he was doing about fifty-five mph (eighty-eight kph) in his grey Citroen BX when he heard the sound of a skidding car behind him. He remembers he was approaching the exit from the tunnel and glanced into his offside wing mirror. He says he saw the Mercedes sliding at a forty-five degree angle to the central island and traveling at a high speed, perhaps ninety mph (145 kph), its headlights lighting up the eastbound lane.

Mohammed added: 'I continued to look in the mirror and saw the Mercedes straighten itself up and head back in the right direction. Then, immediately, I heard a huge noise and saw a piece of the car go flying as the car smashed into the central pillar.' Mohammed made no mention of any other vehicles being involved.

Souad told a similar story. When she heard the noise she turned around to look through the back window. 'I saw a big Mercedes heading sideways across the road onto the island and strike a concrete pillar. Our car was about thirty or forty yards in front of the Mercedes at the moment of impact.... After this first impact the vehicle pivoted around and smashed into the other pavement.' She said she saw the driver's body slumped over, and then other traffic, and then maybe six or seven vehicles, passed the wreck.

Souad saw none of these overtake their car, and she does not know if any of them stopped, but the alleged presence on the scene of so many other motorists within split seconds of the impact clashes with almost all other testimony.

Jean Pascal Peyret, president of a marketing company, had that night taken his family to dine at the highly rated Hotel Bristol and, just before midnight, they set off for home in Versailles in their dark blue Saab. He said he was driving at fifty mph (eighty kph) up the exit ramp of the Pont de L'Alma tunnel when he heard two sounds of a crash, the second much louder than the first, and he thought they came from the street above.

He said that a few seconds later, his car was passed by a motorbike with a sole rider wearing a white helmet and a dark jacket. He appears not to have noticed Mohammed's grey Citroen BX, and it is difficult to judge who was nearer to the accident. Both witnesses were at the wheel of darkish cars, a factor that assumes importance in other testimonies.

Oliver P. and Clifford G. are professional chauffeurs. That night they were strolling over a patch of grass at Place de la

Reine Astrid (inevitably dubbed the 'grassy knoll') on their way home when they saw a Mercedes speeding towards the tunnel entrance. The two witnesses were only fifty yards away and Oliver estimated the speed of the limousine to be ninety mph.

He said a motorbike was following close behind and there was another vehicle in its way: 'The Mercedes was preceded by a car, the type I can't identify. It was dark colored and was trying to slow down the Mercedes,' he told the investigators. 'The Mercedes changed gear to get round the other car and after it entered the tunnel there was the sound of a massive collision.'

As one of the first witnesses to be interviewed on August 31, Clifford told a similar tale and had a little more to say about the motorbike. This part of his testimony had enormous initial significance. He said there were two people on the bike and one was snapping pictures of the Mercedes. He claimed to have seen the camera flash going off as it sped past.

Then his memory began to play tricks on him. Re-interviewed by Judge Stephan in mid-September, he said he could no longer be sure there was a pillion passenger or be sure of any camera flashes. A piece of seemingly hard evidence that at least one paparazzi contributed to the buildup of the accident had to be marked down as unreliable.

More useful is the evidence of student David L., walking with his girlfriend and her parents less than a hundred yards from the tunnel mouth on the grass-covered island beside the expressway. They saw the Mercedes in the left-hand, fast lane, speeding towards the tunnel. A second car was in the right lane as the Mercedes entered the tunnel, and it was pursued by a motorbike carrying a driver and pillion passenger. Some of these witnesses thought the Mercedes may have struck the car. Then they heard the noise of the crash.

Benoit B. was heading east towards central Paris with his girlfriend Gaelle L., in the opposite direction from the Mercedes, and heard the noise of tires screeching and then 'a little impact.' He too was interviewed within hours of the crash and seemed to have had a clear view of the last seconds: 'I saw in the opposite lane two vehicles. The first, a dark colored saloon, accelerated brutally at the moment the Mercedes, that was following in the same lane, the right lane, lost control.

'I saw it slide, strike a pillar—then spin around and hit the wall to end up facing in the opposite direction.' I think the Mercedes was driving very fast and struck the saloon and lost control.' Benoit says a motorcycle or Vespa then slowed down and then accelerated past the crashed car.

Gaelle thought the saloon was a Renault Clio or a Super 5 and that it was driving rather slowly. 'It hindered the Mercedes, which was coming at high speed.' She was not sure whether the two vehicles made contact but the couple's testimony of a dark car playing some role in the accident could not be shaken by the detectives.

Gaelle said that the little car accelerated on seeing the crash: 'I don't know what became of it.' Perhaps no one will ever know. She may have confused the timing of events and actually seen either Mohammed or Peyret's vehicles, ahead of the crash. Or she may have had a crucial sighting of the yet-undiscovered mystery driver.

Equally mysterious is the still-missing motorcyclist. The most intriguing evidence on this point came from François Levistre, also called Levi, a former harbor pilot aged fifty-three who unlike most other witnesses was happy to talk to the press. He told Reuters news agency that his view of the crash was also in his mirrors: 'I saw the car in the middle of the tunnel with a motorcycle on its left, pulling ahead and then swerving to the right directly in front of the car. As the motorcycle swerved and before the car lost control, there was a flash of light. But then I was out of the tunnel and I heard, but did not see, the impact. I immediately pulled my car over the curb but my wife said, "Let's get out of here. It's a terrorist attack!"'

Levistre said he saw a big motorbike with two riders speed from the tunnel. But in his account of the crash he made no mention of seeing anything of Peyret's or Mohammed M.'s cars. Before he was interviewed by police, who apparently dismissed his account initially, he had told it to Bernard Dartevelle, Mohammed Al Fayed's lawyer in Paris, who quoted the story as evidence that at least one paparazzo had impeded the Mercedes.

Doubts emerged about that interpretation when Levistre was questioned for a Granada TV documentary. He said the light was much more powerful than a camera flash gun. Granada demonstrated a special piece of equipment called an antipersonnel device, which sets of a bolt of light in split second that blinds and disorients the victim. It is available commercially for £260 ($430). Levistre said he saw something like that.

He also claimed to have seen a big motorcycle with two riders emerge from the tunnel immediately after the crash. If true, this may be the same mystery motorcycle seen by other witnesses like David L. and Clifford G. But other witnesses only added to the confusion.

Brian Anderson, a businessman from California, was in a taxi traveling west when he was passed, he says, by the Mercedes, followed closely by two bikes. One was trying to get in front of the Diana's car. Thierry H., a Paris businessman, said he was passed by the Mercedes pursued 'by four to six motorcycles.' They were trying to get round the car and they were driving 'aggressively.'

In none of these reports was there any suggestion that photographers on the bikes were attempting to take pictures. In fact the paparazzi were to claim later that it was not their ambition to take any pictures at that time; they merely wanted to discover where the couple would be spending the night. In any case, they claimed, they were losing the target, being a mile or more behind at this stage, and hounding no one.

The single-motorbike theory, however, was subscribed to by Grigori R., twenty-nine, a photographer who was traveling east. As he entered the tunnel in his VW Passat, he heard an enormous crash. His witness statement continues: 'The cars [in my lane] hit their brakes and I slowed down and turned on my warning lights. At that moment I saw a big car in the opposite lane that had just been immobilized. I only saw the last split second of its movement. I saw a motorcycle moving in the same direction as the Mercedes. It was a rather large motorcycle with a round yellow headlight. I had an impression of something white but I cannot say whether it was a helmet or a petrol tank.'

Grigori said he was fairly sure there was only one person on the bike. It took off 'very rapidly after passing in the way I have described.' He said there was no time for it to stop but the driver braked sharply before continuing. He said there was no other vehicle near the Mercedes in that period.

One thing is clear. The early stories from witnesses gave the police little help. Martine Monteil, head of the Criminal Brigade, produced an initial report on September 1, bemoaning the lack of clarity. It read: 'None of the testimony so far received permits us to establish whether a vehicle could have been sufficiently close to the Mercedes to the point of touching it or interfering with its trajectory. Among the elements to consider in explaining this accident, we should note the following: the vehicle was moving at excessive speed; the chauffeur did not regularly drive this type of vehicle (powerful and heavy); the vehicle, according to maintenance records, seems to have been in perfect condition (repairs and tests made in June 1997); and the toxicology analysis on the driver showed a blood alcohol level of 1.87 g/l and 1.74 g/l.'

The suspicion was firmly directed at Henri Paul, but could there have been extraneous factors that contributed to the accident? Examination of the car and mysterious paint marks on the bodywork was well underway by late September, by which time two new witnesses had come forward, for the first time making reference to a white Fiat Uno.

George and Sabine D. told how they crossed the bridge above the Pont de L'Alma tunnel at 12:25 A.M. and drove west to join the expressway as it exits the tunnel. Suddenly they were overtaken by a white Fiat Uno. The driver was 'European' and brown-haired, about forty, and there was a large Alsatian dog in the back of the car. What drew George and Sabine's attention to the car was the vehicle's erratic progress. It was zigzagging; the driver was looking intently in his mirror and he swerved to the right in front of them to park on the hard shoulder. They said the car's exhaust was faulty and it backfired.

As a result, a British lawyer, Gary Hunter, forty-one, was prompted to come out into the open. He told the *Sunday Times* that he saw what he took to be a fleeing car from the window of his third-floor hotel room less than 100 meters from the crash at the Alma tunnel. 'I went to the window and saw people running towards the tunnel,' he said. Seconds later he saw a 'small, dark car' turning from the area by the tunnel exit and roaring down the rue Jean Goujon, the street below his hotel.

'My own feeling is that these were people in a hurry not to

be there,' Hunter added. 'I am confident that car was getting off the scene. 'It looked quite sinister. I can't recall the type of car but it was a small dark vehicle. It could have been a Fiat Uno or a Renault.' And the car was being shadowed by a second, a white Mercedes—yet another tantalizing and untraced vehicle.

There was one final witness from whom everyone wanted to hear. Trevor Rees-Jones, twenty-nine, the bodyguard and only survivor of the crash, was by September 19 well enough to give evidence to Judge Stephan. There were fears that he might have suffered serious head injuries and memory blocks caused by the shock of the high-speed accident, or by anesthetics used in a string of operations to rebuild his face.

The French radio station RTL said the bodyguard's voice had been reduced to a murmur because he had been given a tracheotomy and three titanium screws had been inserted to repair his broken jaw. Nevertheless, he was able to piece together some of the story, though it only added to the mystery.

Asked if he knew whether the Mercedes, carrying Diana and Dodi, was being followed when it left the Hotel Ritz, Rees-Jones told the investigators, 'There were two motorbikes and one car ... I do not remember the route. It seems to me that there was one white car with a trunk that opened at the back.' He said the car was following them when the Mercedes left the Ritz, 'it crossed the street when we left and then it followed us.'

As the months passed, Rees-Jones' memory recovered somewhat and the *Daily Mirror* was granted a scoop interview with the active assistance of Mohammed Al Fayed, his employer. Rees-Jones now said he could remember snatches of what happened as though his memory was switching on and off. He could now recall lying in the car after the crash and hearing Diana groaning and calling Dodi's name. But despite attempts by investigators to prompt his memory, he has no recollection of the period immediately before the crash. Whether the white hatchback had clung to the Mercedes up to the fatal moment remained unknown.

Perhaps surprisingly, Rees-Jones has a vivid memory of events before they departed the Ritz and it is clear he respected the man chosen to drive them. 'I knew Henri Paul from the other times I had met him at the Ritz,' Rees-Jones told Piers Morgan, the editor of the *Mirror*. 'My impression of him was that he was a professional man who knew what he was doing. I'd seen him drive the car behind me from the airport on the afternoon of the day before the accident and saw nothing that said he was a poor driver.

'He seemed perfectly competent to me. He was driving the backup car and I checked fairly regularly. Both me and another member of the security team, Kes Wingfield, were very satisfied with what we saw.'

Rees-Jones said there was nothing untoward about Paul's behavior before they set out on the journey. 'If there had been, Kes or I would have picked it up straightaway. That's what we are trained to do. But he seemed perfectly normal to both of us. He sat at the bar drinking some yellow liquid (pastis) that I assumed was nonalcoholic.... As far as I was concerned, Paul was on duty and that was that. I had no reason to suspect he was drunk. He did not look or sound like he had been drinking. He just seemed his usual self.'

Rees-Jones also said that the idea that Dodi was some sort of speed freak and would have encouraged Paul to go faster and faster was out of character. Clearly there was puzzlement in Rees-Jones' mind that Paul could have suddenly turned into a reckless maniac, again out of character, and willfully caused so much carnage.

In response to a Channel 4 documentary broadcast in June 1998, accusing Paul of being drunk and reckless, Rees-Jones was prompted to issue a further statement through his solicitor. It read: 'As is clear from the video evidence from the security camera, Henri Paul appeared perfectly normal ... Mr. Rees-Jones would not have allowed the Princess of Wales or Dodi Fayed to be driven by anyone he knew or suspected to be drunk.'

However, facts are surely facts. There is the evidence of the blood tests and of Paul's driving manner. The pack of photographers were apparently left far behind when Paul left the Place de la Concorde and accelerated onto the expressway. The Gamma Picture Agency bike rider, Stephane Darmon, said he went 'almost supersonic.' Another said he drove like a gangster.

It is a mystery why none of the other occupants of the car urged caution. Perhaps they did, and were ignored—a surprising piece of insubordination. However, no one will ever know, and that still leaves open the possibility that Paul was not the master of their fate—that another more sinister factor lay behind the most notorious car crash this century.

Chapter Thirteen

Royal Reaction

Although in the days, weeks, and months following the crash there has been much analysis of the impact on the Royal family of the events in the underpass at the Pont de L'Alma, most analysis has been merely speculative, since the Royal family have, probably quite reasonably, never considered it necessary to discuss their reactions publicly. What *has* come under scrutiny is not so much their reactions as their actions.

The reactions of Princes William and Harry cannot reasonably be doubted, as the bond between Diana, Princess of Wales, and her sons was openly close and loving. It was a tactile relationship, and uniquely different from that experienced by Royal children for prior generations. The sudden, harsh news coming in the early hours of the morning would have been devastating in the extreme. But what about the rest of the family?

To continue the speculative analysis of their feelings, we can ask: Did they throw their hats skywards, shouting 'Yes!' as they punched the air? Were they jubilant and triumphal that this troublesome, semidetached Royal member was dead? Of course not. In any case they are all far too well controlled, reserved, or introverted, for such an outward show of emotion.

Yet surely there might have been a flooding sense of relief? Did the name Camilla come jumping into Prince Charles' head as he heard the news, even before the realization of the dreadful task ahead of telling the children? Was there a sense of relief, tempered with some regrets, for the Queen and the Duke of Edinburgh that suddenly the danger of an Arab stepfather for the young Princes was now nothing more than a bad dream—and not the nightmare it might have become?

In any case, their first action was to withdraw into themselves, pulling down the shutters—a retreat from the world and prying eyes. In the seclusion of Balmoral, their Scottish castle halfway between Ballater and Braemar on the A93 in Aberdeenshire where the Royal family spends high summer indulging in the traditional pastimes of fishing and shooting, they anticipated sitting out the final 'Diana Drama' until forced to leave for the funeral. But the apparent safety of the environment into which they withdrew proved quite inadequate to protect them from a situation which was without precedent in the history of royalty. Rapidly their calm, quiet, and dignified mourning was overtaken by increasing confusion and perhaps family conflict.

A mixture of these emotions must have preceded the extraordinary decision to take the two young Princes to morning service at Crathie Church on the day of their mother's death. This involved a drive along public roads, exposing the youngsters to scattered mourners who had gathered along the route and also to the lenses of professional photographers who were, even on an occasion which could hardly be more sensitive, still on their predatory business.

It is no surprise that both boys looked pale and exhausted. If the enforced trip to the church was intended as a lesson in stoicism and tradition or as a demonstration to the world that it was business as usual for the Royals, it looked like an ill-judged and arguably insensitive decision that day and makes no more sense in retrospect, even if the youngsters were given the choice of not attending, as was later claimed. This is especially true as the service remained unchanged, making no reference to the death of the Princess and even including jokes by the Scottish comedian Billy Connolly. Did they try to smile at the Minister's jollity?

Earlier, news of the crash had been telephoned to Prince Charles and the Queen within an hour of the event, with reports that Dodi and the driver were dead, but that the Princess and her British bodyguard, an employee of Mohammed Al Fayed, so disliked and distrusted by the Royals and their advisors, were still alive. The lines remained active throughout the night with details regularly relayed from Paris to the Scottish highlands.

As the ambulance carrying the Princess was driven slowly through the Paris night to the Pitié-Salpêtrière hospital, there must still have seemed a chance, from a distance, that she would survive. At 3 A.M. in Scotland, 4 A.M. in Paris, the final bulletin reported her death. The Princes were not told until several hours later, although Prince William is reported to have said later that he awakened constantly during the night with feelings that something was wrong.

So by the time the Princes were taken to Crathie Church they had known of their mother's tragic death for just a few brief hours. A bulletin was issued by staff at Buckingham Palace and reported by early morning TV news programs saying: 'The Queen and the Prince of Wales are deeply shocked and distressed by the terrible news.'

Following church, the Prince of Wales drove himself to Aberdeen to meet Diana's sisters, Lady Sarah McCorquodale and Lady Jane Fellowes, and to bring home the body of his divorced wife. In one news report that night it was claimed that wrangling within the Royal family had started even before church. The Prince was said to have been forced to overrule officials to use an aircraft of the Royal Flight to make the visit to Paris and to bring home Diana.

Further controversy was already intruding on grief. Following the divorce settlement, the Princess had been stripped of her Royal title and consequently, according to accepted protocol, was not entitled to a State funeral. The same report suggested that bending this rule, and thereby flouting convention, was not seen as an option by the Royals, and indeed may not even have been considered a possibility at this stage by stern traditionalists in the family such as the Duke of Edinburgh. The alternative was for a private funeral organized by the Spencer family from their home at Althorp in Northamptonshire.

The problems went even deeper. It has been reported that there was opposition from certain members of the family and officials (who included Sir Robert Fellowes, the Queen's Private Secretary and the brother-in-law of the Princess), to allow the body of the Princess to be laid in State in any of the Royal Palaces, including her own home in Kensington Palace. It would appear that the Prince received virtually no help on the Sunday of the crash. He had to organize every detail of the flight to Paris and the sad homecoming himself, even to the point of telephoning ahead to insure there would be a wreath placed on the coffin.

If Prince Charles was disturbed by these problems, and if in Paris he barely appeared to know what was going on, his feelings were matched in intensity by those of Earl Spencer, who was reported on Channel 4 News to be 'enraged' by suggestions of a private funeral. This early dispute was said to have colored all later dealings with the Palace. It was also reported on the same news program that the decision to allow the Princess to lie in the Chapel Royal at St. James's Palace and for her to have a public funeral at Westminster Abbey was made only after a telephone conversation between Prince Charles on the flight deck of the BAe 146 aircraft taking him to Paris, and the Prime Minister, Tony Blair, in London.

At this very early stage in the unraveling drama there appeared to be two camps facing each other across the trenches of progress and conformity, with Prince Charles lined up with Earl Spencer and the Prime Minister on the one side, and the Queen, the Duke of Edinburgh, and the fervid traditionalists among their advisors, such as Sir Robert Fellowes, on the other. Having Lady Fellowes, the Princess's sister on board the Royal Flight, must have made for an uncomfortable, as well as immensely sad, journey.

In the Channel 4 program, newsreader Jon Snow reported that at one point Prince Charles invited Robert Fellowes to 'impale himself on his own flagstaff.' As this reported conversation took place prior to the demand by the public to know why the flag on Buckingham Palace was the only one in the country not to be flying at half mast, it was unlikely to have been a flag-related discussion.

Later there were firm denials of Snow's comments by all the parties involved, including Earl Spencer, the Prime Minister's press office, and the Palace. But Jon Snow refused to retract his story, saying his 'sources are very reliable, nongovernmental, but very close to the court circle.' It is also undeniable that there was anger in Earl Spencer's attitude up to and including the ceremony in Westminster Abbey, and the Prime Minister's office has let it be known in private briefings that Tony Blair was advising the Royals throughout.

If there was squabbling among those wrestling with the many problems of etiquette, protocol, and tradition involved in the arrangements for the funeral, there was no doubt about the immediate and overwhelming response of the British people to the death of their beloved Princess. In the early hours of the Sunday morning, long before most of the world had learned of the Paris tragedy, the 'flower power' tribute began.

Single blooms, especially white lilies, posies, and bouquets, were laid at several sites in London. It started slowly, with just a trickle of people, to the front gates of the Princess's home at Kensington Palace, to the front of Harrods, the Knightsbridge department store owned by Dodi's father, Mohammed Al Fayed, and to the gates of Buckingham Palace, although initially the Buckingham Palace offerings were turned away by the authorities.

For the news-hungry media these moving tributes, which included cards, candles, poems, framed photographs, balloons, and even soft toys, became a symbol of the love and affection which the British people harbored, and indeed still continue to display, for Diana, Princess of Wales. And as the trickle of flowers became a flood, which continued to dominate the news reports, they also became a beautiful, fragrant, and yet slightly ominous harbinger of change for the Royal family.

The 'Diana Years' had already witnessed the most important changes in the institution of royalty for generations. Layer upon layer had been peeled back from the once untouchable monarchy, exposing it to examination and criticism which earlier would have seemed unimaginable. A once great symbol of power and authority, it had been scrutinized during the 1980s and 1990s in every little detail by the press and politicians, especially those with republican leanings.

And very often the Establishment had been found wanting. Changes of fundamental importance followed: suddenly their accounts were open to scrutiny by Parliament, their side door at Buckingham Palace was open to any nosy tourist who wanted to saunter through the state apartments, their yacht was ditched, and even the tax man was getting his nose in the trough. Maybe the greatest shock to the institution had been the discovery that a once slavishly loyal public also thought change was necessary. The Queen decided to pay for repairs and restoration work from her own resources following fire damage at Windsor Castle.

At the time of the Paris crash, feelings of dissatisfaction with the establishment of monarchy existed in the country more as an undercurrent rather than as a noticeable desire for social change. As a trend, it had been accelerated by the behavior of the younger Royals. The marriages of three out of the four children of the Queen had ended in divorce, while the fourth remained determinedly unmarried. Their antics were followed by a wider audience than just the British press. The *New York Times* has been moved to describe the family as 'the world's most dysfunctional royal fairy-tale.'

The emotional trauma which engulfed the world in the aftermath of the Diana tragedy inevitably found the spotlight focusing on the family once again. Their actions of retreating in grand seclusion at Balmoral, seemingly unaware, as usual, of the mood of the country, attracted a hostile response from the public and was for once a genuine reaction and not something massaged into prominence by the tabloid press. As the populace continued to show its love and respect for the lost Princess, it could see nothing which mirrored its emotional shock reflecting back from the Scottish highlands.

The mounds of flowers continued to grow during the week between the crash and the funeral, until they became memorials in their own right. In the days following Diana's death, the grief in London, as in every town and village, was palpable; one could almost feel the sorrow in the air as children and their parents gathered in public displays of loss and emotional despair.

This was totally at odds with any previously perceived ideas of the British character. Strangers were to be seen comforting each other, the old helping the young, and the wealthy and dispossessed joining together in paroxysms of despair. Even some of the most hard-bitten cynics were moved to tears upon reading the loving tributes taped to the railings of Kensington Palace by grieving members of the public.

The sense of growing anger that this grief was not reciprocated by the Queen and her immediate family created an anti-monarchist surge throughout the country which was exacerbated by the realization that the only flags in the country not at half-mast were those above the Royal palaces, with Buckingham Palace a particular source of offense, appearing on TV almost nightly.

If this all created a menacing attitude towards royalty, then the situation deteriorated even further in the furor over Diana's 'royal' title. This squabble was created at least partially by the press, who indulged in a little kite-flying with suggestions that their readers were demanding the posthumous return of Diana's royal status, stripped from her at the time of the divorce.

The Queen might have agreed to such a move, which would have been both unconstitutional and quite without precedent, but the gesture was, however, firmly rejected by the Princess' brother, who in a warm, affectionate tribute to his sister declared: 'She needed no royal title to continue to generate her particular brand of magic.' He made it clear to Sir Robert Fellowes that even if a posthumous restoration of the title, relinquished voluntarily by his sister, were offered, the Spencer family would not accept it. In a later statement, a palace spokesman announced that the Spencer family had been consulted and 'their very firm view was that the Princess herself would not have wished for any change to the style and title by which she was known at the time of her death. The Spencer family itself also did not wish for it to be changed.'

In the midst of this public aggression and private confusion the Royal party was eventually forced to abandon its plan to remain in Scotland. Their decision, it has been reported, was helped along by intervention from Prime Minister, Tony Blair, who when still in opposition had several meetings with Diana. He had been so impressed by her rapport with the needy and disadvantaged that he was ready to champion her cause to became an unofficial ambassador on the international stage.

He had already made a most moving and perceptive address to the nation on the morning of her death, when speaking without notes from his Sedgefield constituency he told the world: 'She touched the lives of so many others in Britain and throughout the world with joy and comfort. How difficult things were for her from time to time, I'm sure we can only guess at. But people everywhere, not just here in Britain, kept faith with Princess Diana. They liked her, they loved her, they regarded her as one of the people. She was the People's Princess and that is how she will stay, how she will remain in all our hearts and memories forever.'

His comments captured the mood of the nation immediately and echoed around the world, and in their simplicity cast unfavorable comparisons on the tributes from the more staid members of the Establishment.

With their return to London 'by popular demand' and the announcement of a 'a unique service for a unique person' the Royal party went a long way to restoring their image. They were helped in a number of ways. Thousands of people were waiting for up to twelve hours in seemingly endless lines to sign just five Books of Remembrance. An increase in the number of books to forty-three eased the pain. Then, of course, they were helped immensely by the mature and caring way in which the young Princes carried out their duties. While the Queen and the Duke of Edinburgh went out to meet the crowds clustered outside Buckingham Palace, the two boys went 'walkabout' in the crowds at Kensington Palace.

In a warm and friendly way reminiscent of their mother, they charmed the crowd. Prince William in particular showed a remarkable similarity to the late Princess, especially in his mannerisms and rather shy smile. As he thanked the crowds, leaning out to grasp people's hands, it was already possible to see the beginnings of a transfer of love and adulation from the mother to the son. He handled himself with great dignity, even when many women kissed his hand before bursting into tears.

From the balcony of Buckingham Palace on the eve of the funeral, the Queen addressed the nation. With the TV cameras whirring she said: 'What I say to you now as your Queen and as a grandmother, I say from the heart. First, I want to pay tribute to Diana myself. She was an exceptional and gifted human being. In good times and bad she never lost her capacity to smile and laugh, to inspire others with her warmth and kindness. I admired and respected her for her energy and commitment to others, especially her devotion to her two boys.'

On the following day, the Princess was buried on an island in the grounds of the family home at Althorp House following the largest public funeral the country had experienced since the death of Winston Churchill. An emotional address by Lord Spencer, in which he attacked the world's press and took more than a few side-swipes at the Royal family and all those whom he believed had contributed to her troubles, brought unprecedented applause, starting in the multitude watching the ceremony on giant screens in Hyde Park and spreading into Westminster Abbey itself.

Elton John, a close personal friend of the Princess, bravely sang his tribute song, 'Candle In The Wind' specially rewritten for the Princess, live in the Abbey, before rerecording it in the studio to become a massive best-seller, raising millions of pounds for the Princess' Memorial Fund. On the long final journey from London to Althorp, the hearse and the roads themselves were strewn with flowers in a unique and unforgettable tribute to the lady who had captured every heart, and to whom no one wanted to say goodbye.

Diana, Princess of Wales, had rattled royalty in many ways. She was offered no training, either in the duties of a future Queen or help in dealing with press, and despite facing pressures for which no amount of training in 'royalty' could have prepared her, she still displayed a greater talent for the work than any other member of the family. She brought about changes which were clearly difficult for the Prince of Wales and his own family to understand, still less control or emulate. She cast aside their pomp and ceremony, their protocol, and those elements of tradition which create a barrier between royalty and commoner.

Despite their resentment of her popularity and success, it may eventually prove that she did more to strengthen the Royal family than anyone else. The signs are already evident that the young Princes have inherited her charm and warmth, and the greatest changes may yet come through them. How sad it therefore is that there is a lingering suspicion among many that the full story of how and why she died cannot be laid to rest as Diana was with such dignity. Had she lived it is very much open to doubt that she would have sided with those who say, 'forget the conspiracy theories; there is no doubt it was an accident.'

Chapter Fourteen

Demand for Answers

I f Henri Paul had survived the impact of the head-on crash he would certainly have faced many searching questions once his injuries had been patched up. He was over the limit, according to the blood tests. He drove at a very fast speed along an urban clear-way with a thirty-one-mph (fifty-kph) limit. He may have taunted the paparazzi outside the rear entrance of the Ritz. To claim innocence, the onus would have fallen on him to show he was not drunk, that somehow the blood tests and certain witnesses had given a false picture.

Kes Wingfield and Trevor Rees-Jones pronounced their employer's driver to be sober but, being loyal Ritz security men, their testimony would have carried little weight. As allegations swirled around about Ritz cover-ups of the events that evening, much of it irrelevant to the question of Diana and Dodi's deaths, the heavily edited Ritz videos were also called into question. It has been alleged that at least one video is missing and that Paul may look less abstemious in any segments that might have been left on the cutting room floor.

More damning are those more neutral observers who have accused Paul of being well over the limit. One is Frederic Lucas, another chauffeur who came forward as this book went to press. He said he handed over the Mercedes 280 to Paul just before he drove off with his passengers. 'Paul was in very high spirits. No one could have been in any doubt that he was intoxicated,' Lucas said.

There is little doubt that Paul had two shots of Ricard in the bar, but that is not enough to account for him being three times of the French limit. However, it is clear some Ritz employees believe he exhibited all the signs of having been drinking heavily. One said he saw Paul stagger. They may not have liked their acting security boss, but would they have made such a story up?

With the crucial evidence of the blood tests, it is surely likely, if not certain, that Paul would have faced manslaughter and reckless driving charges had he survived. One can imagine how the hatred of the world would have focused on the small, amiable Breton. As it is, there will be no trial of Henri Paul, no sifting of minute detail, and no certainty he would have been found guilty.

As we have learned, the blood tests themselves are being challenged now that the significance of high carbon monoxide levels is better appreciated. Those with suspicious minds will wonder why the families of the crash victims—notably Paul's and Dodi's next of kin—have been refused samples of blood so that they could conduct their own analysis. And they will point to the strange fact that whereas a strict ban on releasing details of the French investigation was imposed from the outset, the blood test results were announced within hours of the crash.

If the blood tests are false, then no straightforward explanation will be credible.

Those who want blood in a more metaphorical sense may be content to see charges laid against some of the paparazzi. Nine of them and a courier rider were placed under formal investigation for allegedly failing to assist at the scene and for manslaughter. However, any trial will be a limited affair, disregarding many important aspects of the larger mystery, notably whether any other foul play was also involved.

Successful prosecution of the paparazzi is also doubtful because of the lack of evidence that any of them were close to the car when it crashed. Those witnesses who saw bikes near to the Mercedes as it approached the tunnel do not appear to have identified any of the accused photographers, who claim to have arrived at the scene well after the car struck the tunnel support.

There is even doubt about how badly the snappers behaved at the crash scene. The police were critical and American tourists Jack and Robin Firestone maintained in countless TV interviews that they swarmed over the car—even lying on the hood to get a better view. But there is little evidence they hindered medical efforts.

Legal action aside, the photographers cannot be absolved of blame entirely, for there is no question that Henri Paul was pressed to drive with great haste because they were, initially at least, on his tail. For most it is business as usual in Paris, following around other celebrities with perhaps just a little more respect for their feelings.

With no clear scapegoats, the deliberations of Hervé Stephan and his team will assume great importance. Their opinion of what happened will of course be well informed. But following one of the biggest police inquiries ever mounted in France, it will have to be hedged with a number of caveats. As time passes, the loose ends have increased in number as promising lines of investigation fail.

Over the months, as the official investigation progressed, Stephan must have prayed his team would discover a white

Fiat Uno—one of the remaining great mysteries—and it is easy to imagine how it would have transformed the inquiry. According to reports in early 1998, this was the car that was just entering the slow lane of the tunnel when the Mercedes tried to speed past. In the process, it is postulated, the Fiat was struck by Paul's vehicle, shedding bits of debris.

The Fiat then apparently kept pace with the Mercedes, preventing it from overtaking. Then, as the Mercedes crashed into the thirteenth pillar, the Fiat driver weaved his or her way past the stricken vehicle, and all the debris on the road, and callously made off for the tunnel exit.

Seconds later, or so it is argued, the same car was seen by George and Sabine D. after they had crossed the roadway above the Pont de L'Alma tunnel. They were driving west to join the expressway as it exits the tunnel when a white Fiat Uno came zigzagging and backfiring out of the underpass.

The two witnesses remembered that the hatchback's driver was European, brown-haired, and aged about forty, with a large Alsatian dog in the back seat. They recalled with remarkable precision that the incident happened at 12:25 A.M., the moment when the Mercedes ploughed into the pillar. What they described seemed to link up with the discovery of Fiat Uno taillight fragments near the tunnel entrance. However, it is just as possible there may be no connection.

The couple took six days to come forward and tell the police what they had seen and they could easily have made a mistake about timing. As discussed before, almost all other witnesses either describe seeing a dark second car in the underpass before the impact or no car at all. By the summer of 1998 therefore, Stephan's team were said to be highly skeptical that the existence of a Fiat Uno was a worthwhile line of inquiry.

Certainly the most exhaustive search had failed to find a trace of it, or its driver, or the dog. The paint flakes found on the Mercedes had been of limited help, as the same paint was used on many other models of car. In any case, whatever the car they were looking for, if it existed at all, may have been resprayed or destroyed.

Forensic science had therefore failed to produce the hoped-for solution. Hollywood soaps aside, this is not unusual. The tests at the investigators' disposal only rarely produce conclusive proof, and they are often more useful in eliminating irrelevant evidence.

No scientist could say for certain if any foreign paint on the Mercedes' body work was deposited fractions of a second before the crash or, for example, earlier that same day. It is known that the car had been parked in the Ritz car park unattended, and no one examined it to check the bodywork was perfect before it carried its illustrious passengers to their deaths.

Not only is the existence of the white Fiat Uno therefore in doubt, it is equally uncertain whether the Mercedes was hit by any other vehicle. The tiny bits of debris from Paul's car found near the tunnel entrance might simply have been flung there as a result of the final impact.

It must also gall the investigators that no one saw the crash in clear detail, and there is therefore no chief witness on which the investigation could rely. The most crucial witnesses of all were the occupants of the Mercedes. Three perished and Trevor Rees-Jones has regained no memory of what happened in the crucial moments up to impact. The events described by other witnesses are in so much conflict that it is impossible to piece together a coherent story.

People saw glimpses from the opposite carriageway. People

arrived on the scene seconds later. People were overtaken and heard the crash in the distance. People got a snatched view in their wing-mirrors.

In desperation Stephan staged a special reconstruction at the Monthléry Motor Racing Circuit outside Paris in May 1998. The French police said a Mercedes model, like that driven by Henri Paul, and motorcycles and scooters similar to those used by the photographers were put through exercises to collect evidence on acceleration and braking speeds. Watched by gendarmes, police and civilian experts, the tests were expected to provide data to corroborate or refute the conflicting eyewitness accounts of the accident. However, it leaked out that it shed little extra light on what occurred.

In a further attempt to reconcile all these stories, the judge called a 'Confrontation,' a gathering together of witnesses including paparazzi. Lawyers for the bereaved families were able to grill them, but by all accounts it also resolved little. One lawyer who attended offered the opinion that we would never know the answer to what happened in the underpass.

The stories remained unreconciled, adding further fuel to the assassination theory. There are enough suspicious factors to justify belief in a secret plot.

First there is Henri Paul himself, and the £122,000 ($200,000) he had accumulated in his many bank accounts — on a salary of £20,000 ($33,000) per annum. There is his mystery blond friend who has not been identified. And his friend Paul Garrec also reveals he had close contacts with French and foreign spying organizations. It seems he was more than just the acting head of hotel security, and it is conceivable his loyalties lay elsewhere, though how this could bear on the crash is equally unexplained.

Then there are his blood samples, containing 20 percent

carbon monoxide, one of the most puzzling pieces of the forensic evidence. If the blood tests are accurate, was Paul somehow accidentally gassed earlier in the evening or was he deliberately targeted with some device? For those with the right contacts, a commercial assassination kit is sold in South Africa, designed to gas people after they have started their car's engine, and which then melts, disintegrates, and leaves no trace.

It is of course a far-fetched idea, as is the notion that the Mercedes might have been tampered with in some other way, so that a killer could take over control of the car and force it off the road. But the idea that some murderous group could have doctored the car is, as we learned, not only feasible but has happened before. We have the opinion of no less authorities than Sir Ranulph Fiennes, the explorer and former SAS officer, and Sir Peter Horsley, a former Air Marshall who was apparently a victim himself.

Then there is the arrest of Oswald Le Winter—almost certainly a former spook but, equally, a man with a reputation as a hoaxer. Le Winter claimed Henri Paul had been poisoned and his Mercedes tampered with, and produced documents that appeared to prove it. Are they forgeries or was he onto something?

The problem for most people with such a conspiracy theory, even if one can believe it to be credible, is the lack of opportunity. The plan to take Diana in the Mercedes 280 from Etoile Limousines was made only shortly before she began the journey, perhaps within the hour. Nevertheless, the Mercedes had been parked all evening in an unattended part of the Ritz's underground car park. It was simply driven out—by whom is in dispute but it was either a director of Etoile or employee Frederic Lucas—and handed over to Henri Paul, who was waiting on the pavement of rue Cambon with his passengers. And it had been mysteriously stripped of its electronics and repaired a few months earlier. Such factors are the cause of speculation for obvious reasons.

What is also known is that a mysterious clutch of men were seen in the crowd around the Ritz Hotel that night—they appear on the hotel's video recordings. As discussed in detail in the previous chapter, a mysterious motorbike and a second car (either dark or white depending on the witness one heeds) may have played a part in the crash but have never been found. Also there was a sighting of a TV crew filming the crash who have disappeared. If any of these sightings are authentic, people close enough to Dodi and Diana could have been bent on mischief.

And the loose ends do not just apply to missing persons. There were reports that some police radios were mysteriously silent in the minutes of the crash, and closed-circuit TV cameras were reported out of action on the route taken by the Mercedes. The airbags in the front of the Mercedes may have inflated prematurely. Had they been working, the brilliant flash allegedly seen by driver François Levistre might have been explained. As it is, Granada Television in Britain was able to advance the sensational theory it was an antipersonnel device, rendering Henri Paul blind and confused just before he skidded into the thirteenth pillar.

Who would have wanted to harm Dodi and Diana? We have looked at that issue and the answer is not comforting. Peter Scott, the former 'human fly' and lifelong crook, said that highly placed people were out to target Dodi and Mohammed Al Fayed, and he said he warned Diana's mother Frances Shand Kydd as recently as three weeks before the crash. Even if Scott's evidence is disregarded, it cannot be denied that professional assassins are loose in this world, as Sir Ranulph Fiennes has also illustrated. The evidence of a shadowy group prepared to step outside the law to protect the interests of the British Establishment is equally strong.

Diana's fears that she was in danger from a group seeking to protect the interests of the British Royal Family will be echoed by many others until the Squidgygate Affair is fully explained, as well as the assertions of threats of skulduggery by her former close friend James Hewitt. He maintains people close to the Royal Family, and a minor member of the Family, warned him he would be in physical danger unless he ended the relationship.

No one need be in any doubt what might be the motive for any dirty-tricks operation against Dodi or Diana. If she was pregnant, as at one point the letter bearing the name of Dr. Pierre Coriat, chief anesthetist at Pitié-Salpêtrière Hospital, seemed to indicate, it should be a simple matter for the public to be told, but the French and British authorities have conspired to evade that issue too.

Even if the pregnancy stories are wrong, her relationship with Dodi and with his father was close enough to trigger shock waves under Buckingham Palace—and generate acute concern at what effect this might have on a future monarchy with the possibility that a future King might have an Arab stepfather.

Such concerns were of course of limited interest in the Palais de Justice in Paris. In June 1998, Hervé Stephan and his team of investigators were still trying to sort out the mass of conflicting evidence about the crash itself when another distraction intervened. British television began a very public squabble over what their own competing investigative teams claimed to have uncovered.

Granada TV screened its documentary, giving credence to the conspiracy idea and the use of a lethal flash device, and casting doubt on whether Paul was really drunk. On the other hand, Channel 4, its main rival for advertising, took a diametrically opposed view and said Paul was to blame beyond doubt.

It was sad to see groups of journalists from both camps heatedly criticizing each other on a follow-up discussion program. There is an old principle in journalism that it is unwise for dog to eat dog—particularly, as in this case, when there is a lack of coherence in so much of the known evidence. However, it helped to focus public attention on a few of the issues regarding the crash that remained unresolved.

There was much comment after the programs were aired that there is no need for television, the press, and books like this to sift over such matters when the French inquiry will provide the answer in due course. The reconstruction of the paparazzi chase at Monthléry Motor Racing Circuit, and the much publicized Confrontation held by Hervé Stephan, do not, however, inspire confidence, coming nine months after the events they sought to elucidate.

It is of course customary for French investigations to be conducted in secret, as was the Confrontation hearing, but such secrecy is not always helpful. If there had been greater press coverage of the evidence available to the investigation, new witnesses might have come forward and known witnesses might have had their memories jogged. Above all it would have lessened speculation and the dissemination of wilder theories.

Also after the crash there was delay in protecting the accident scene and the integrity of the crashed car itself, which meant that vital evidence could have been removed or planted. It is clear that some witnesses were disregarded, like Eric Petel and François Levistre, only to be hauled in months later after their memory of events would have faded.

The inordinate length of time it has taken for the gendarmerie to complete its checks on the wreck of the Mercedes also raises questions. That this might require well over a year of examination and analysis seems surprising, and it is puzzling that Mercedes' offer of help was spurned. When the time comes for Stephan to pronounce, there is therefore no guarantee his findings will be believed.

Equally hard to understand is the lack of questions posed in Britain about the role of MI5, MI6, and Special Branch. As far back as the Spycatcher revelations in the 1980s, the British public should have realized they are not to be trusted entirely, and that the cloak of secrecy surrounding their legitimate activities can also be used to cover up incompetence and misconduct.

These are organizations that among other duties are expected to protect VIPs, particularly Royals, but apparently they were invisible in Paris in late August, 1997. There has been no public statement, or calling to account, about what their role in this tragedy might have been. Were their agents supposed to be keeping an eye on Diana, either to safeguard her safety or because she was regarded as trouble? The British Security Services must have had their own internal inquest. If that is the case, why have their findings not been shared with the British public to whom they should be answerable?

In the US, the CIA and FBI would surely have been obliged to issue a report. But in Britain there has been silence or evasive answers. The British secret services almost certainly had no hand in killing Diana, but by neglect they may have made a contribution to the tragedy for which they should be called to account.

Was Henri Paul an occasional 'asset' of theirs? Can they

shed any light on the carbon monoxide in his blood and whether the alcohol readings are of doubtful value? Were they stationed in and around the Ritz on the night in question, and were they following the Mercedes as it sped away? Who broke in to the photographic agency in North West London? Almost none of these nor many other questions will be answered because in Britain it simply is not considered 'seemly' to pose them of those who rule us.

Index

Who Killed Diana?

Who Killed Diana?

Index

Who Killed Diana?

Index